Books by Alan Pakaln:

La Festa di San Gennaro - © 2017
(Italian translation: *The Feast of San Gennaro, Little Italy, New York, 1971*)

New York Shadow: Behind The Scenes - © 2018
Photographs
Coney Island, 1965
Night from a Car Window, 1965
The Feast of San Gennaro, Little Italy, 1971
Manhattan, Washington Heights, c. 1972
Bellevue Hospital, 1982
Times Square from a Bus, 2000
NYC Outtakes, 1970 – 2009
West Side, Lower Manhattan, 2018

NYC: B&W: Photographs, 1965-2018 - © 2019
(Black and white photographs, uncoated paper,
first published as *New York Shadow: Behind The Scenes*)

Robot Desires: The Social Behavior of Technology - © 2000, © 2018

We Are The Machine: Only Following Orders - © 2019
(First published as *Robot Desires: The Social Behavior of Technology*)

Invention is the Mother of Necessity - © 2018
(First published as *Robot Desires: The Social Behavior of Technology*)

Into It: Interviews With Work - © 2019

The Feast of San Gennaro

Little Italy, New York, 1971

A Photographic Essay

The People, Food, Activities

The Feast of San Gennaro

Little Italy, New York, 1971

A Photographic Essay

The People, Food, Activities

Alan Pakaln

I put much effort into preparing and presenting this manuscript. I would very much appreciate hearing any comments, including complaints. This is Print on Demand (POD), therefor I have limited control over the quality of production, however, I will attempt to address any problem to the extent that I can. To contact me, even just to say hello, go to: alanpakaln.com

FOREWORD

About the photographer.

By profession, I am a biomedical engineer with many years experience overseeing the application of medical technology in New York City hospitals. By amator (amateur), I am a photographer with many more years experience than my profession.

I was born in New York City (Doctor's Hospital, now a luxury condominium), and have lived and worked in and around NYC all my life. My education in photography began about age 17, and took place in a small dark room, a closet under the stairs leading to the basement of the house I grew up in. I was self taught, and a proud amateur: I traded a commercially driven workday for the play and love of my own taking. That said, my darkroom had two enlargers, one for medium format, and I could produce both color and black-and-white images. And now, like most, I use a digital camera, scanner, and printer.

At each successive residence, a photographic darkroom was built: under an elevated platform bed in lower Manhattan loft, a living room with blackened windows in a 5th-floor walk-up in Washington Heights, and in a spare bedroom of an apartment in Westchester County, NY. I've never been a high-tech enthusiast, but I studied aspects of Weston's and Adams' zone system. I also shot in medium format using a Mamiya, C330, 2 1/4. Still, my favorite cameras were the Nikkormat 35mm and the inexpensive, early point-and-shoot cameras, like a Brownie with 127 film.

CONTENTS

INTRODUCTION

New York City, 1970's

In the early 1970's New York City was beginning a slide into disrepair that would peak in the late 1970's. Even as tenants had begun moving into the new World Trade Center complex, several of the boroughs were losing populations, arsonists torched buildings for the insurance, graffiti was everywhere, crime was up, and the city was broke.

How this all happened is a story in itself, but one thing was clear: the city was not pretty to look at. In New York City, you could say that 1971 represented a lull between storms: the 1960's social revolutions, and the deterioration of the late 1970's.

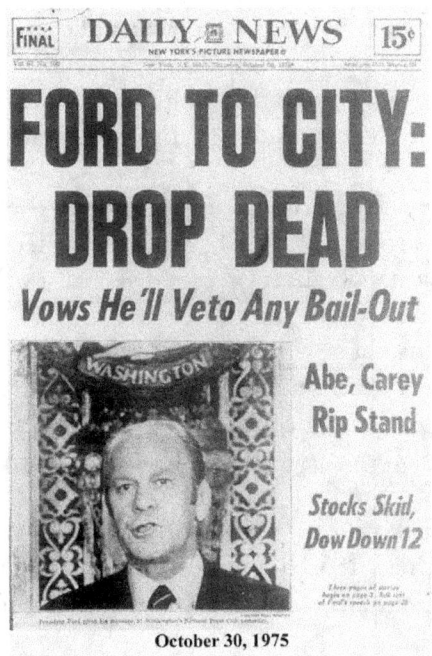

October 30, 1975

The Festival

Recorded histories about The Feast of San Gennaro do not offer much detail regarding the 1960s and early 1970s other than basic facts of its existence. The Feast had not yet been fully media-exposed, and was not very well known beyond local knowledge, visiting relatives, and some adventurous tourists looking for exotic corners of the city.

Prior to the 1960s some photographs and descriptions exist - crime scenes, and other historical accounts - but one could guess that attention to this festival might have been limited due to a society distracted by the war in Vietnam, and politics and people in rebellion. As an attention grabber, The Feast did not scream loudly. That would begin to change by 1974 when, commenting on its size, New York Magazine called the festival "no place for the fainthearted."

Roughly speaking, the area of Little Italy is bordered north and south by East Houston and Canal streets, and west and east by Lafayette and Bowery. By most accounts, the Italian population of Little Italy in the twenty-first century is a fraction of what it was in the twentieth century. Today, that culture is represented mainly by a few restaurants and shops, and also by a festival, The Feast of San Gennaro.

Gennaro, the Bishop of Benevento and the patron saint of Naples, was born around 272 AD. The centerpiece of the festival is really the procession, which expresses the passion and the belief in what the Bishop has come to represent: his faith, dedication, and determination in the face of many challenges. Gennaro's history is a mix of fact and myth stemming from his arrest for visiting a prisoner, his avoidance of punishment, and the representation of blood saved after his execution. It is this vial of blood that forms the centerpiece of the procession on the first day of the festival.

The first festival was in 1926 and has run continuously every September since then. It is now presented by Figli di San Gennaro (Children of San Gennaro), a not-for-profit community organization.

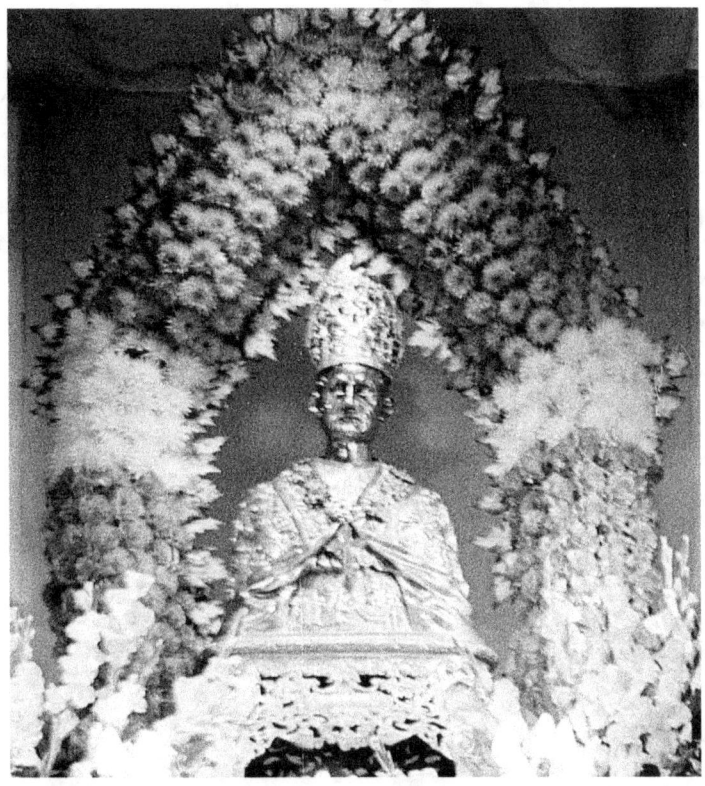

The photographs, September, 1971

What I mostly see when I look at these photographs are the faces of those who made the festival work, faces of a different time, a different era. An era just prior to the Genovese Family, and before Rudy Giuliani interfered, before Mean Streets, and The French Connection. When I look at these faces I see acceptance, acceptance of a person's place, and of the festival's place in the community. It was an era of its own making, one based on hard work and exhibiting what we might now call innocence (In fact, the only indication I could find as to who actually ran the festival is in one of my photographs, Luigi's Pizzeria & Heros, a sign in the window is signed, "THE COMMITTEE.").

It was perhaps 5:30 in the afternoon when I came upon the Feast of San Gennaro in lower Manhattan. I was living nearby at the time and would often wander the streets with my camera, a Nikkormat with Plus-x, black and white film, set at ASA 200. I realized I had little light remaining in the day with which to shoot. I saw many wonderful scenes and began taking pictures, starting at one end of the festival and finishing at the other. Some people thought I was from the press; one person asked if I was from the Village Voice - remember, this was before the festival's extreme popularity and long before everyone carried a camera in their phone!

All photographs were taken in about 45 minutes, which for me was an extraordinary experience. All photographs are shown exactly as they were taken: full-frame, no manipulation.

A Recent Visit

It is November 4, 2017, and I have just returned from a visit to Mulberry Street in lower Manhattan, a main street in the area known as Little Italy. It was a cool fall day, mostly sunny, and a Saturday which means Little Italy was getting its fair share of visitors - shoppers, strollers, eaters, and onlookers, like me. But I'm on a mission: it's been 46 years since I photographed The Feast, and I want to experience the same neighborhood in a new way - with my older eyes and through the lens of a digital camera.

I'm taking the same path I had taken in 1971, and I am also trying to locate Luigi's Pizzeria, or whomever the current owner may be. My Luigi's photograph is one of the few that has any information documenting a specific place, and I thought it might be interesting if I could locate, at least the space it occupied 46 years ago.

I also wanted to publish the 1971 photographs by first grounding the presentation in the present time, to get a further sense of what time can do, and how different not only the scenes look, but also how differently we go about looking. Back then, I was using a single lens reflex camera, black-and-white film, sparingly, to make every shot count. Today it's a digital camera with a rear viewing screen for composing, and no fear of running out of "film."

I may have found the restaurant that is now in place of Luigi's, but I also found what I had read often, that Little Italy, still very much a popular visitor's attraction, has now a fraction of the residential base it once had. All societies and cultures change over time and Little Italy is no exception, however the cultural spirit of this place is still very much alive and present.

The following are some of the photographs I took today. I could shoot in color, of course, but I wanted to relate to the images in the same way I did back then. That is, to emphasize the graphic elements rather than the color, and better relate the two eras visually.

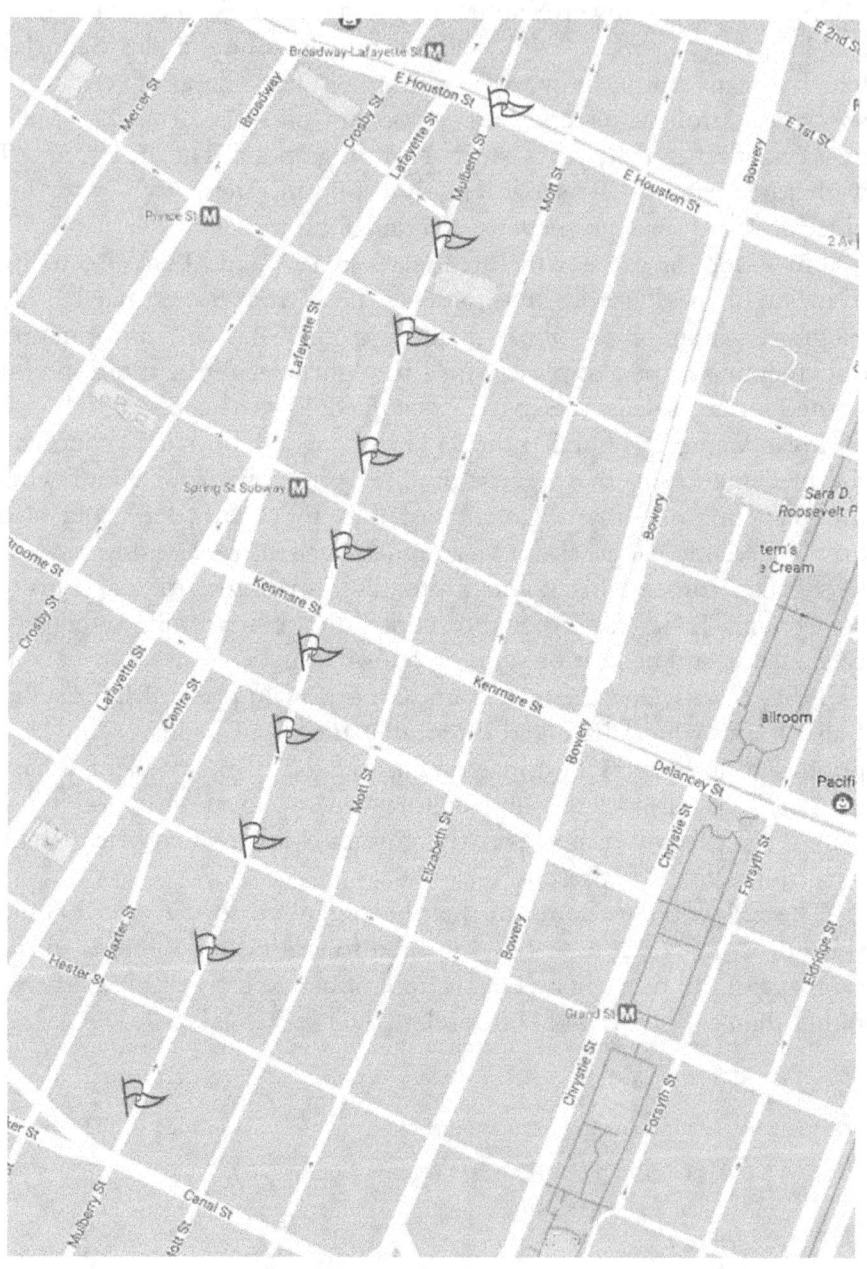

Mulberry Street
Location of The Feast of San Gennaro

LITTLE ITALY, NOVEMBER, 2017

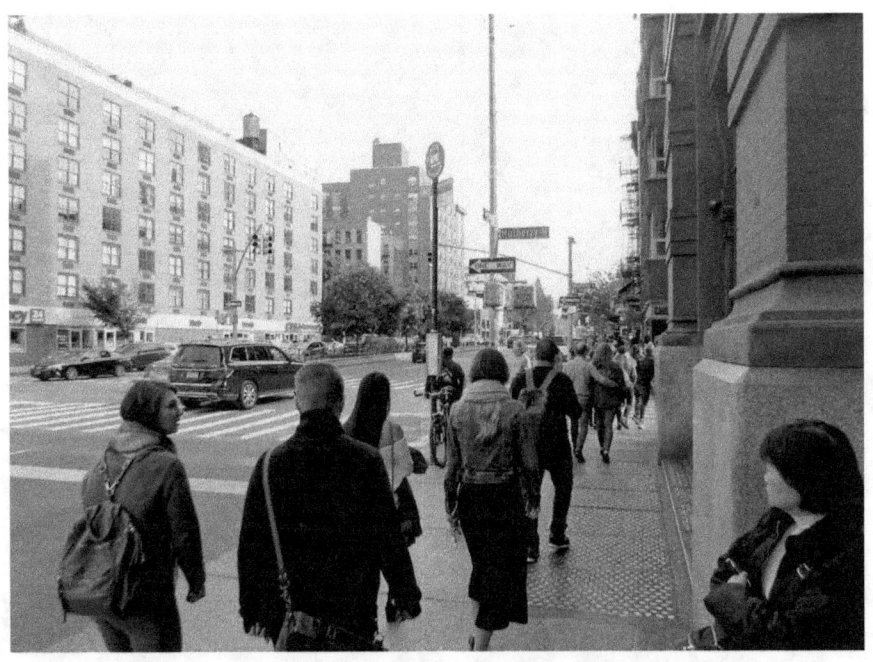

The northern end of Mulberry Street (on the right),
looking east on East Houston Street.

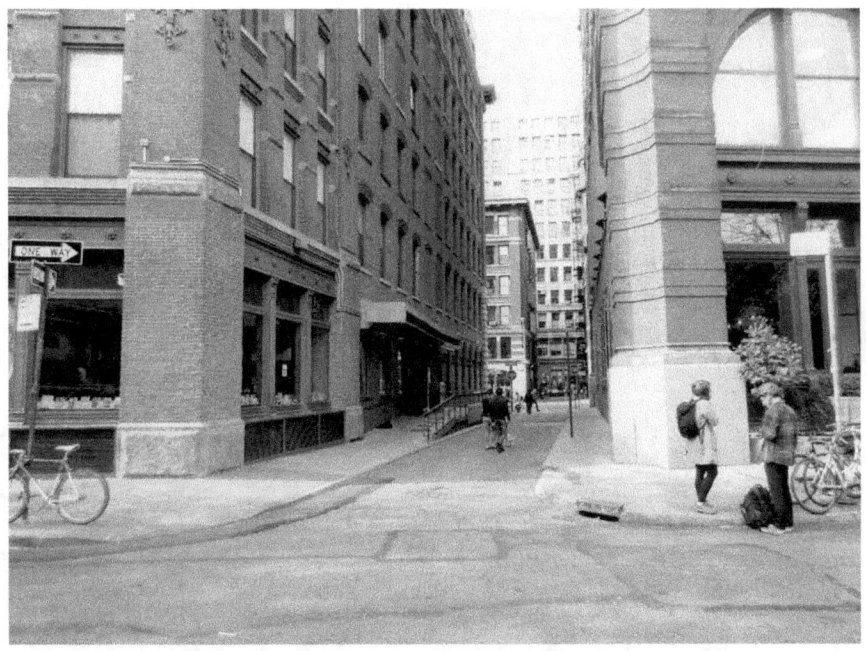

As you turn the corner onto Mulberry Street,
you pass by a very small side street, Jersey Street.

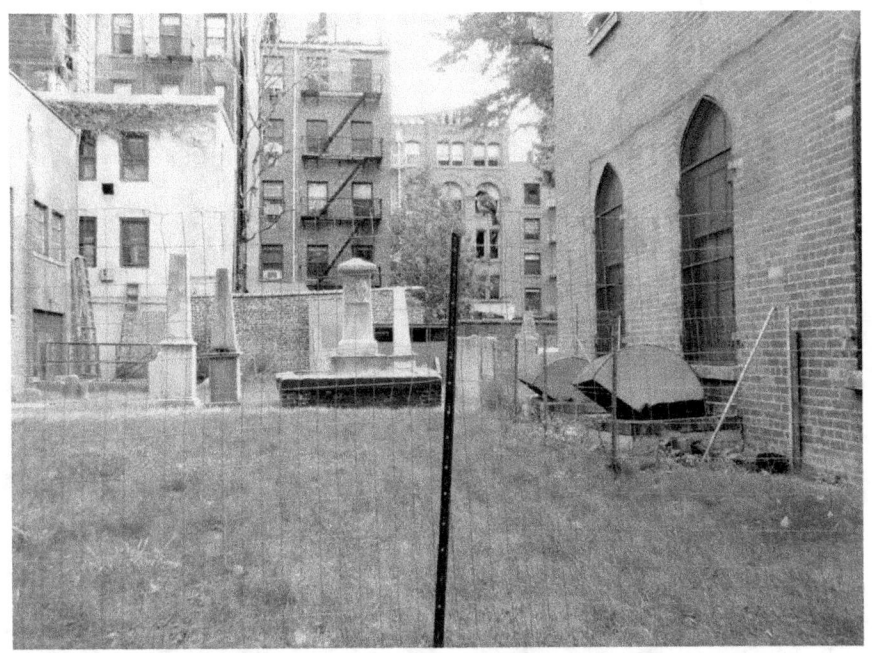

Cemetery next to St. Michael's Chapel

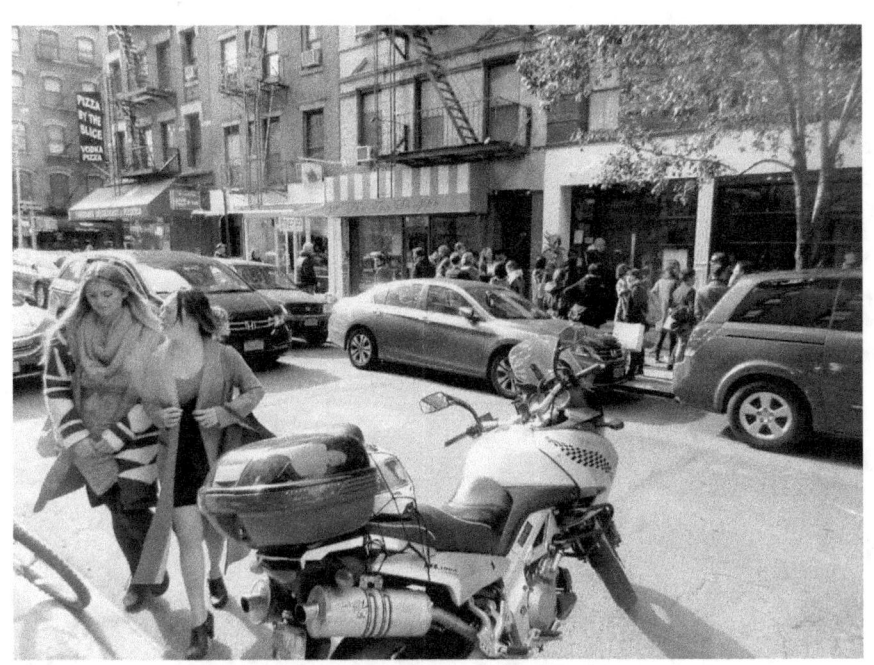

Scene on Mulberry Street

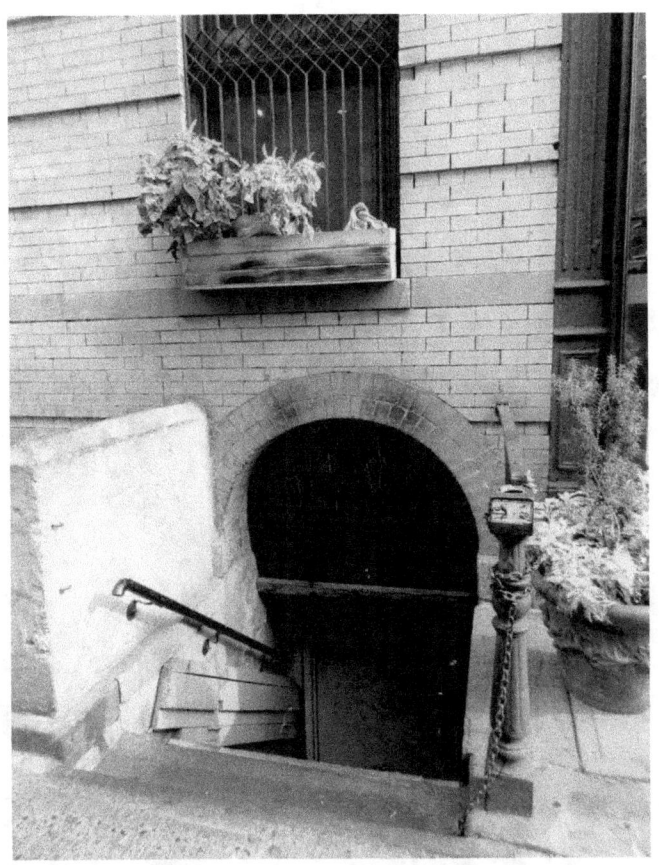

Back Door on Mulberry Street

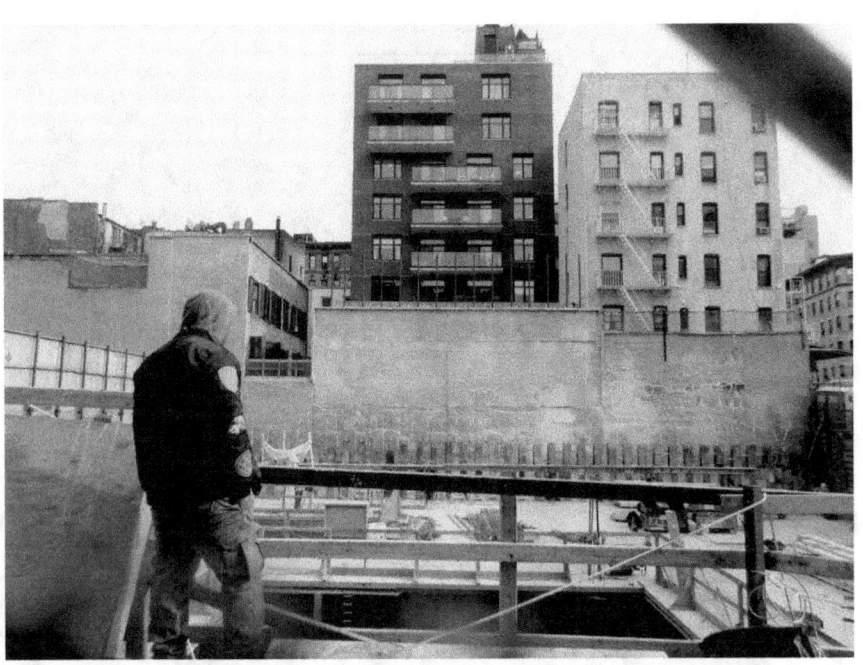

Construction, Kenmare Street & Mulberry Street.

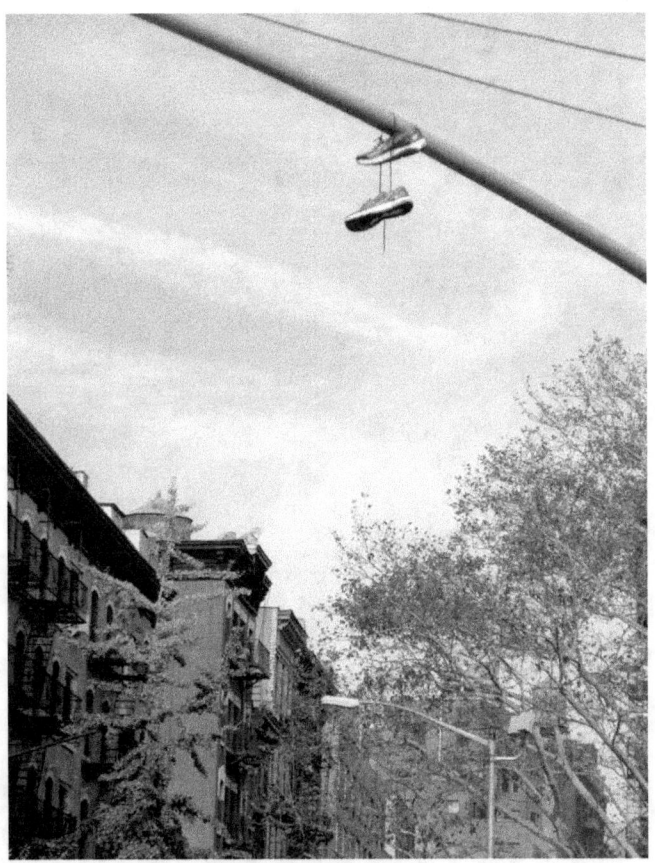

Kenmare Street & Mulberry Street

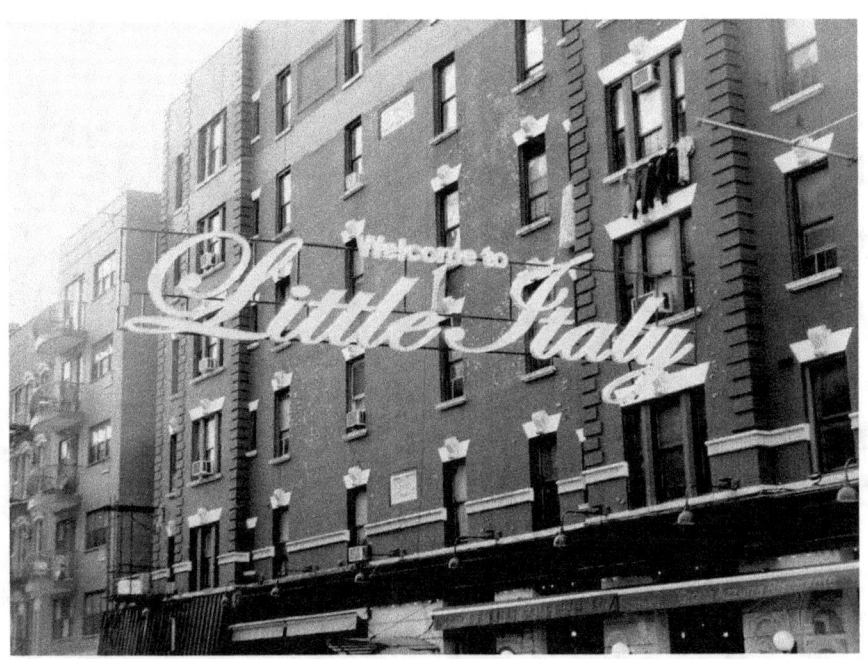

Broome Street & Mulberry Street

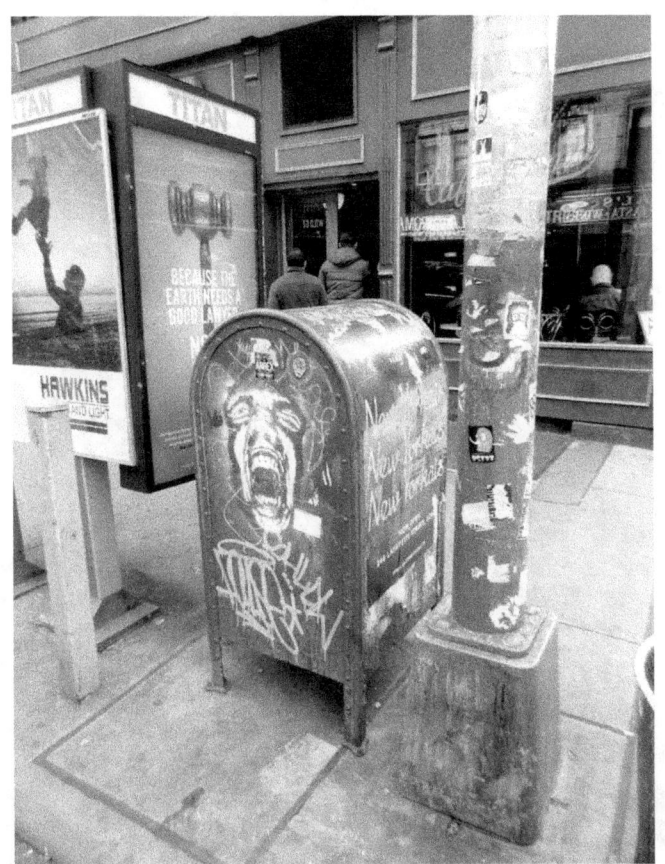

Mailbox Art

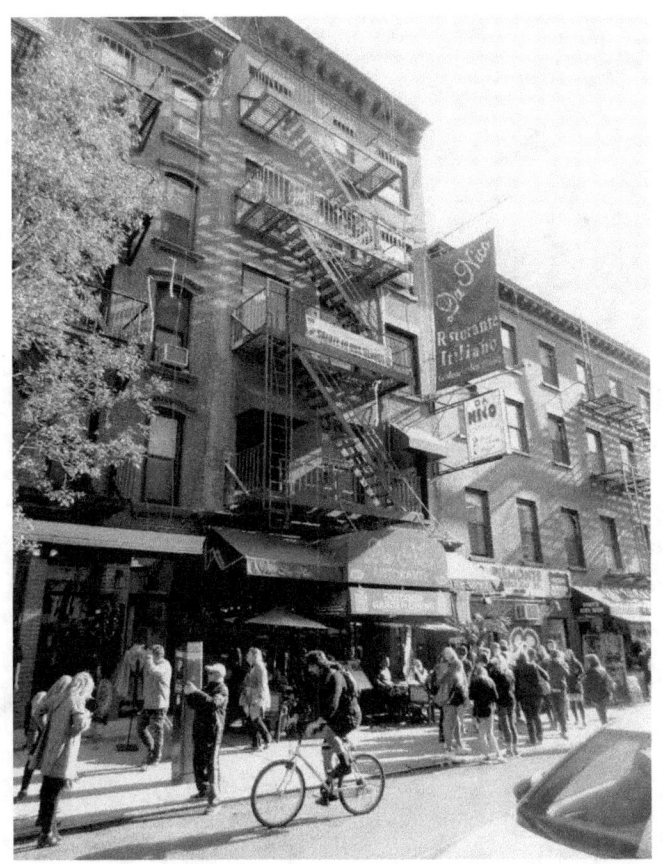

Mulberry Street Scene

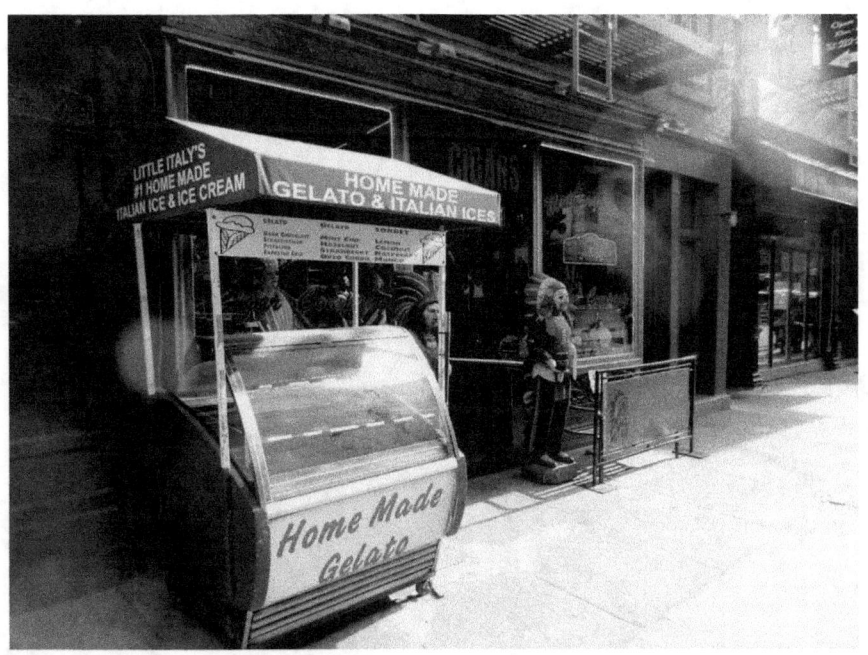

Italian "Indian" Ice

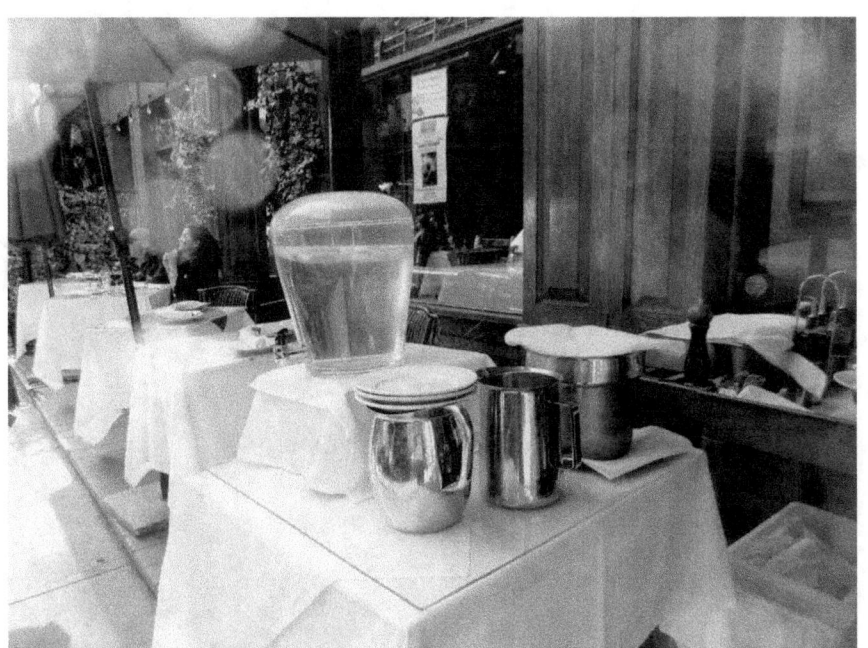

Lemonade

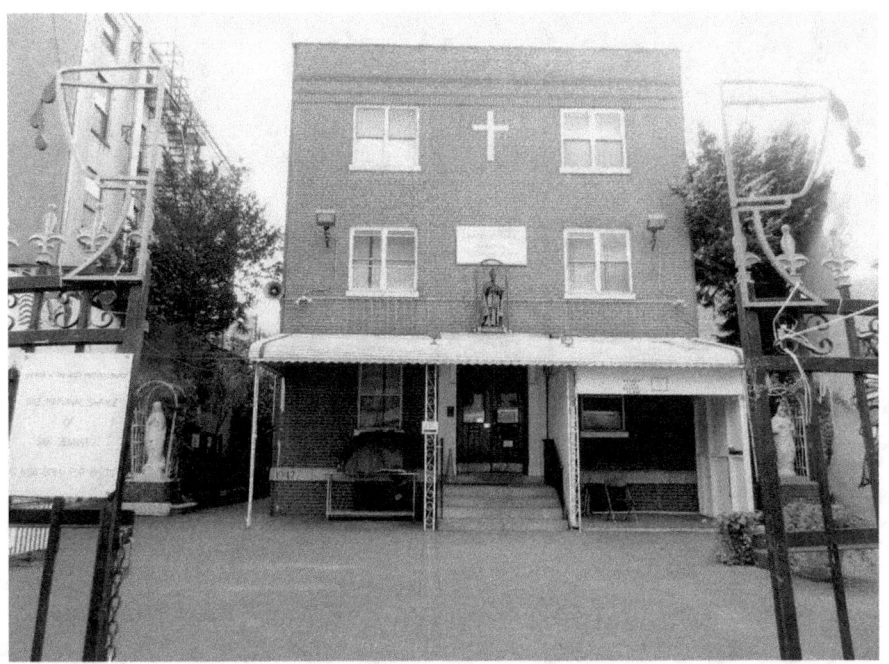

The National Shrine of San Gennaro.

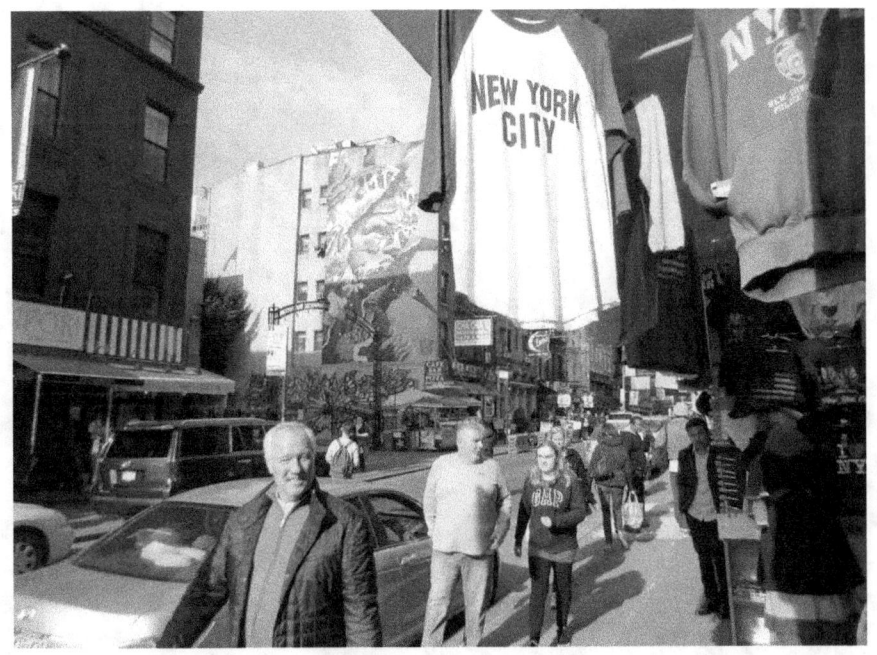

Mulberry Street Scene

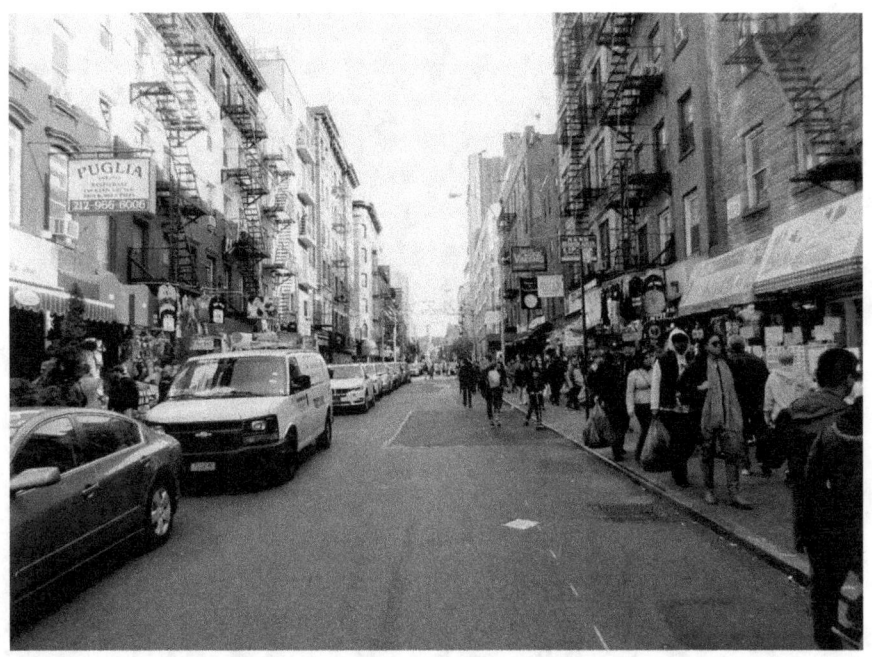

Southern end, Mulberry Street & Canal Street.

THE FEAST OF SAN GENNARO, 1971
The People

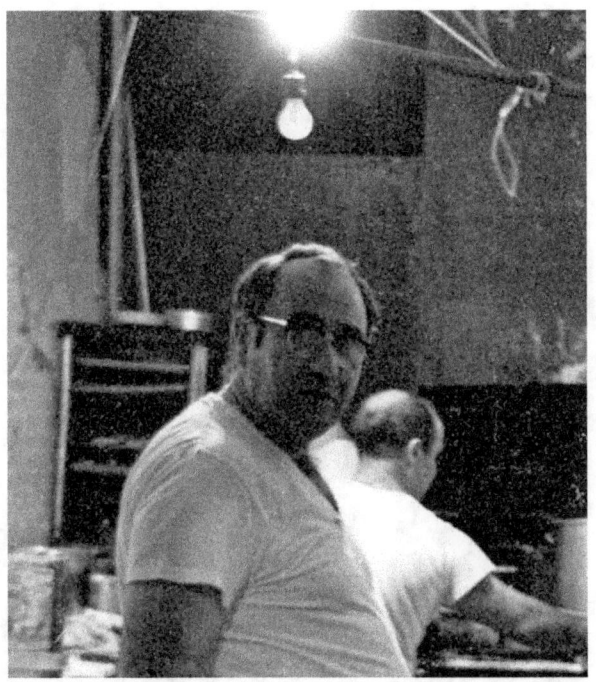

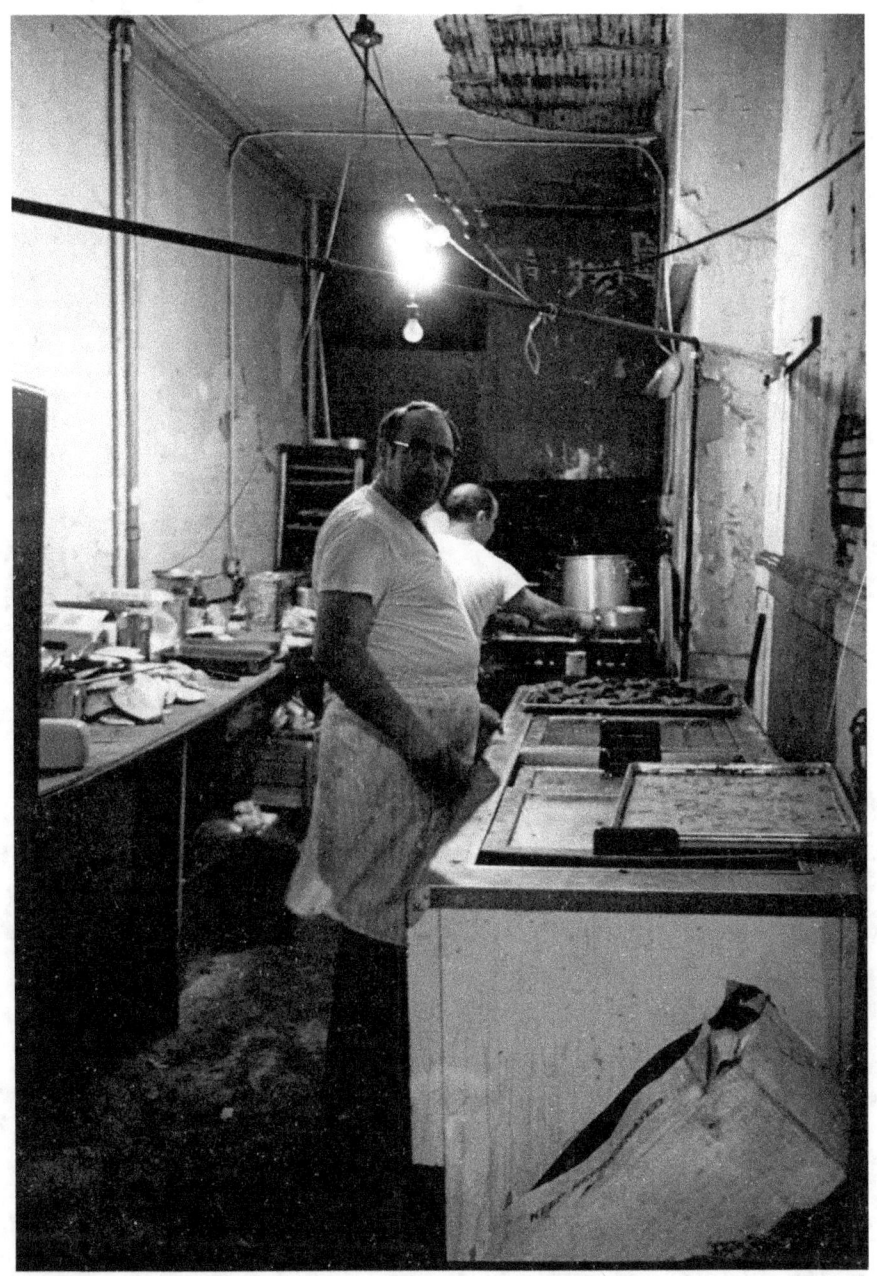

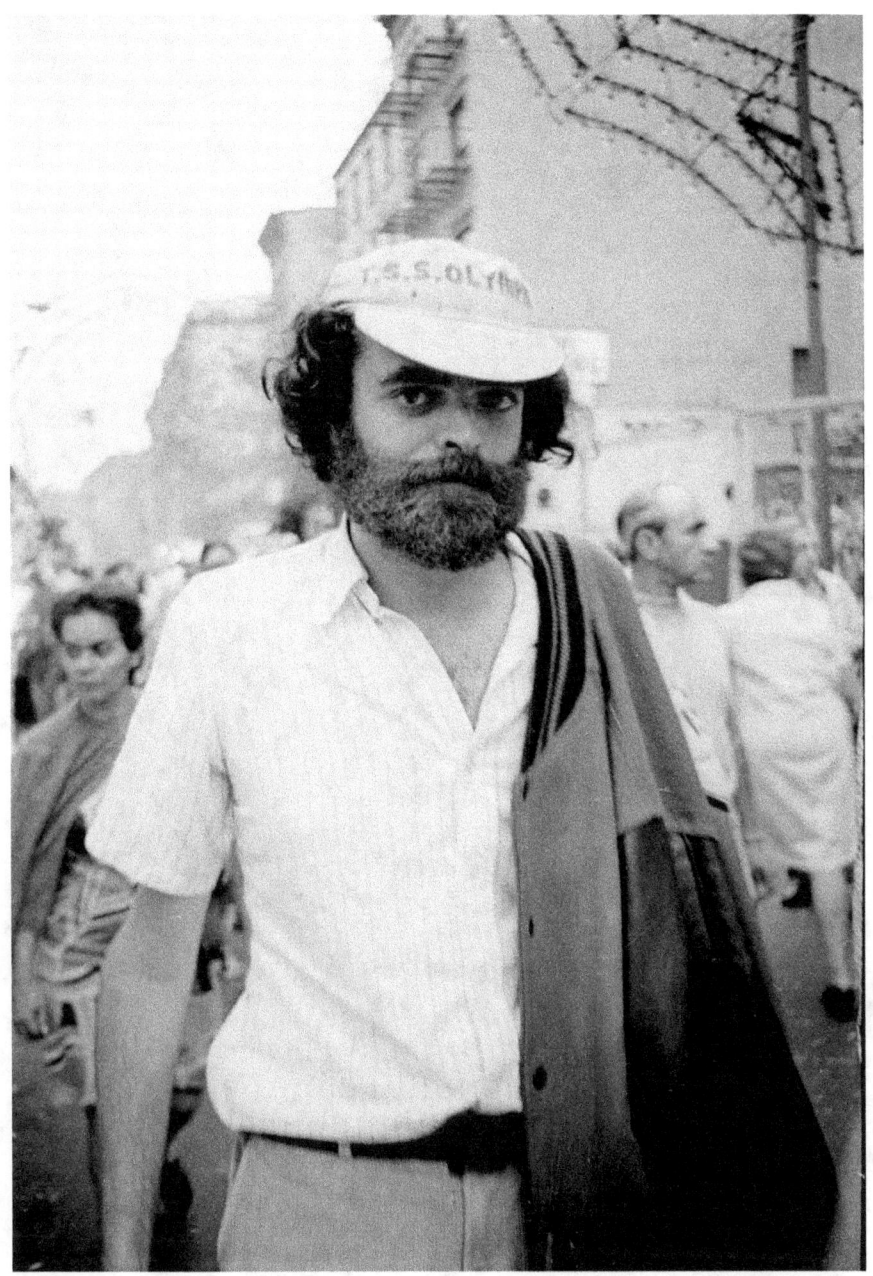

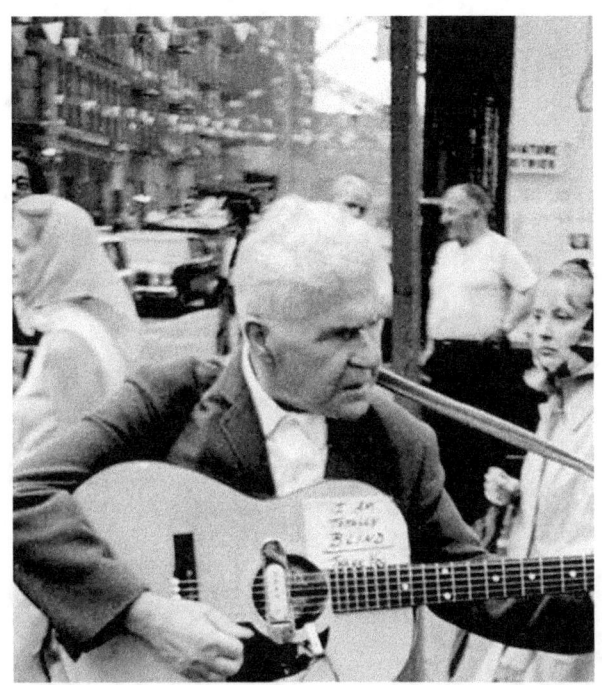

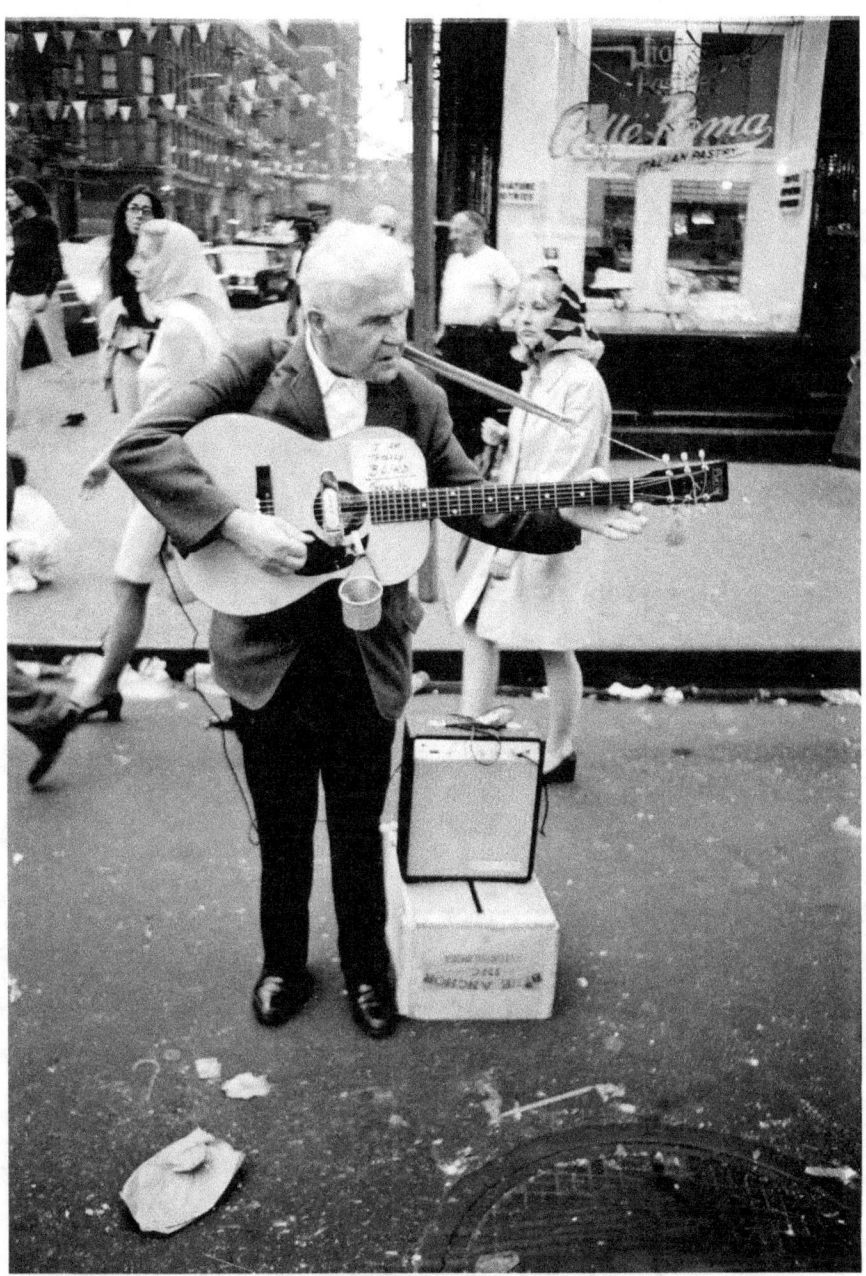

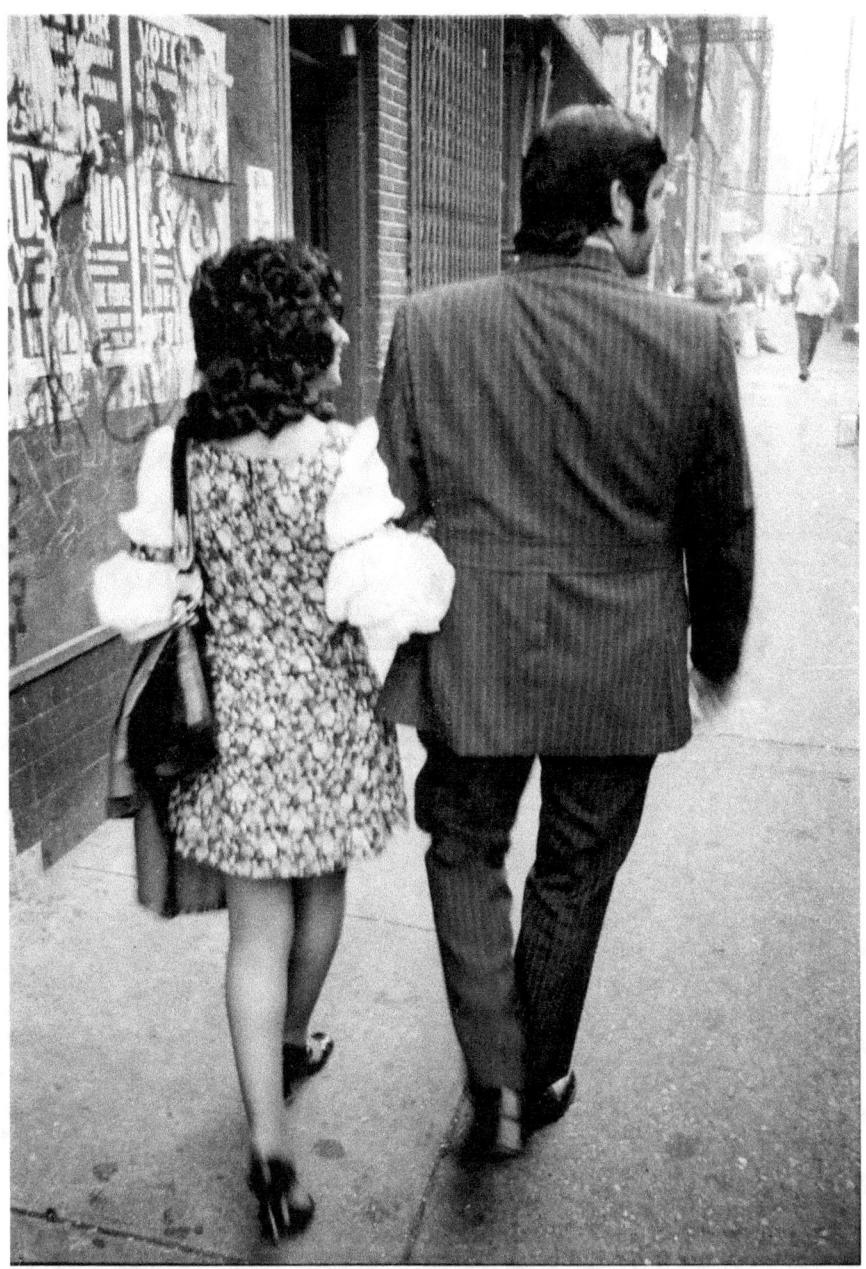

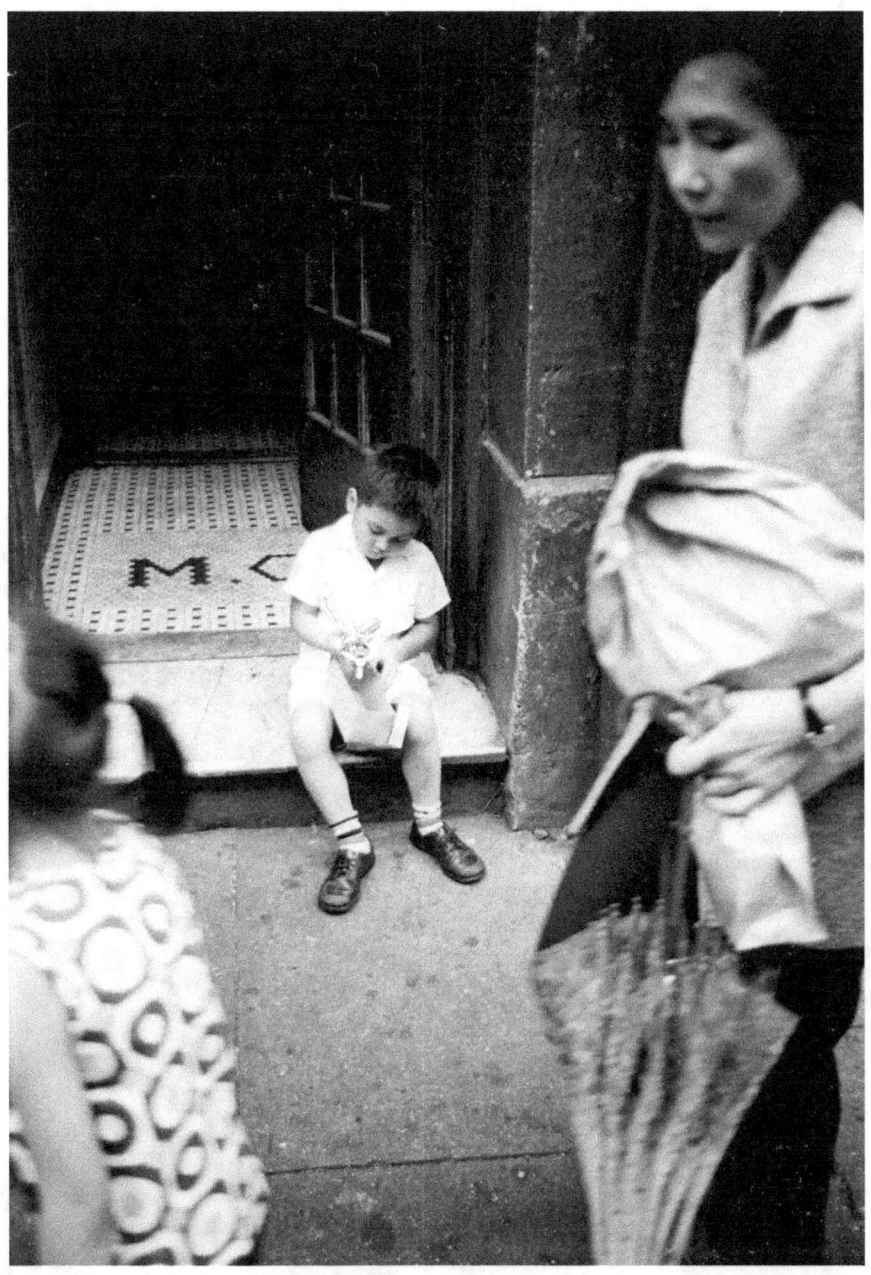

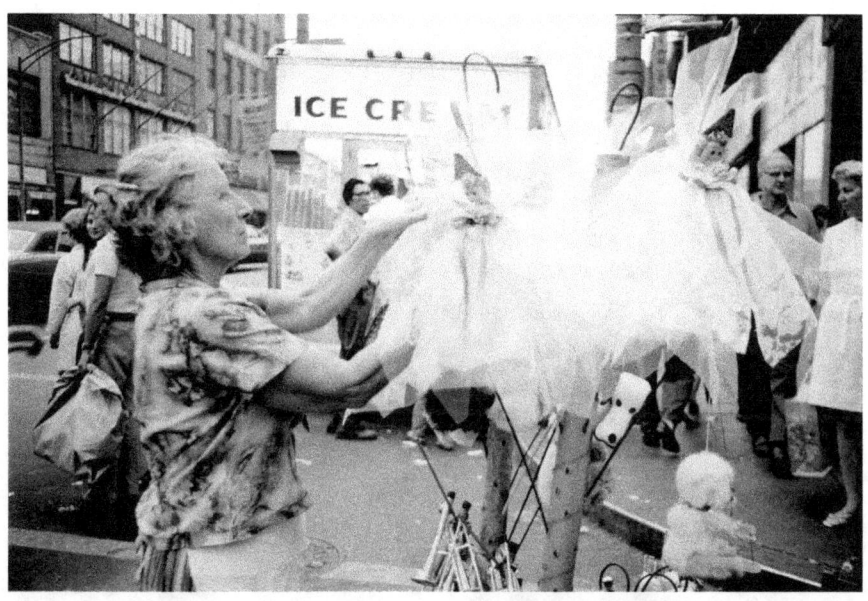

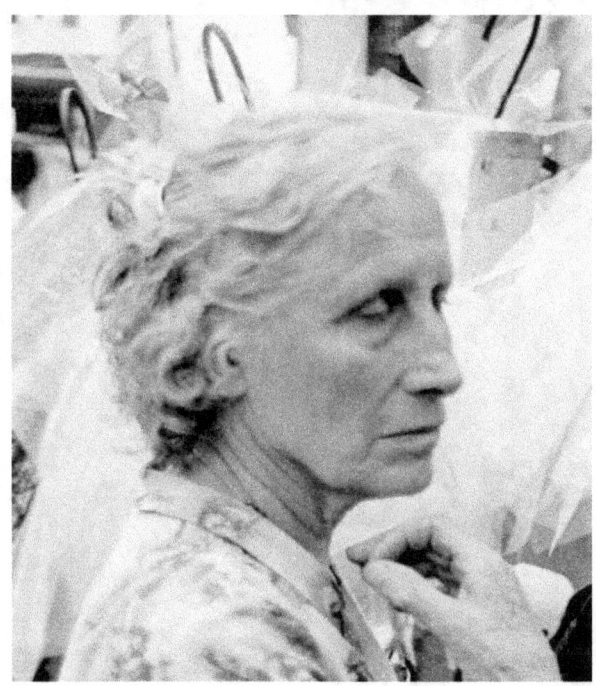

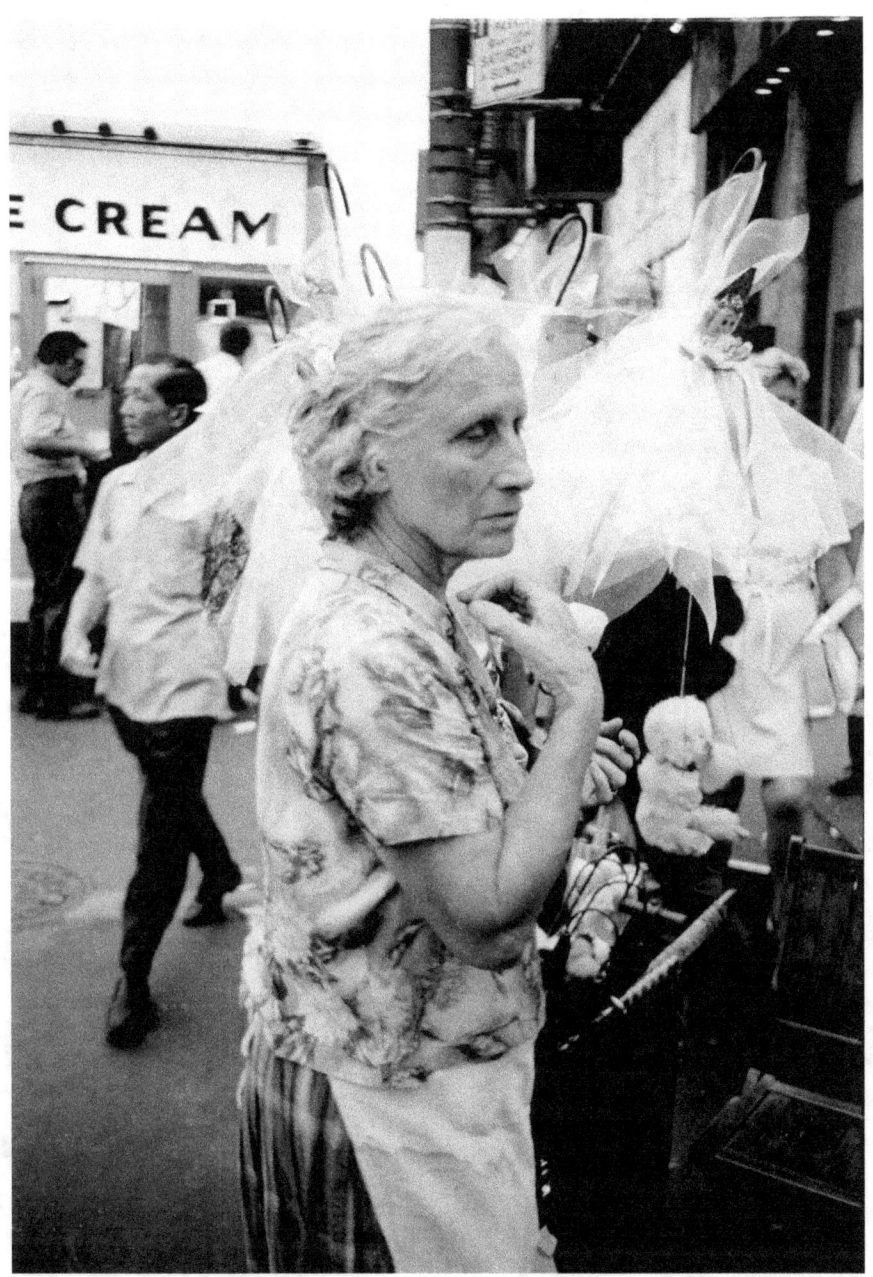

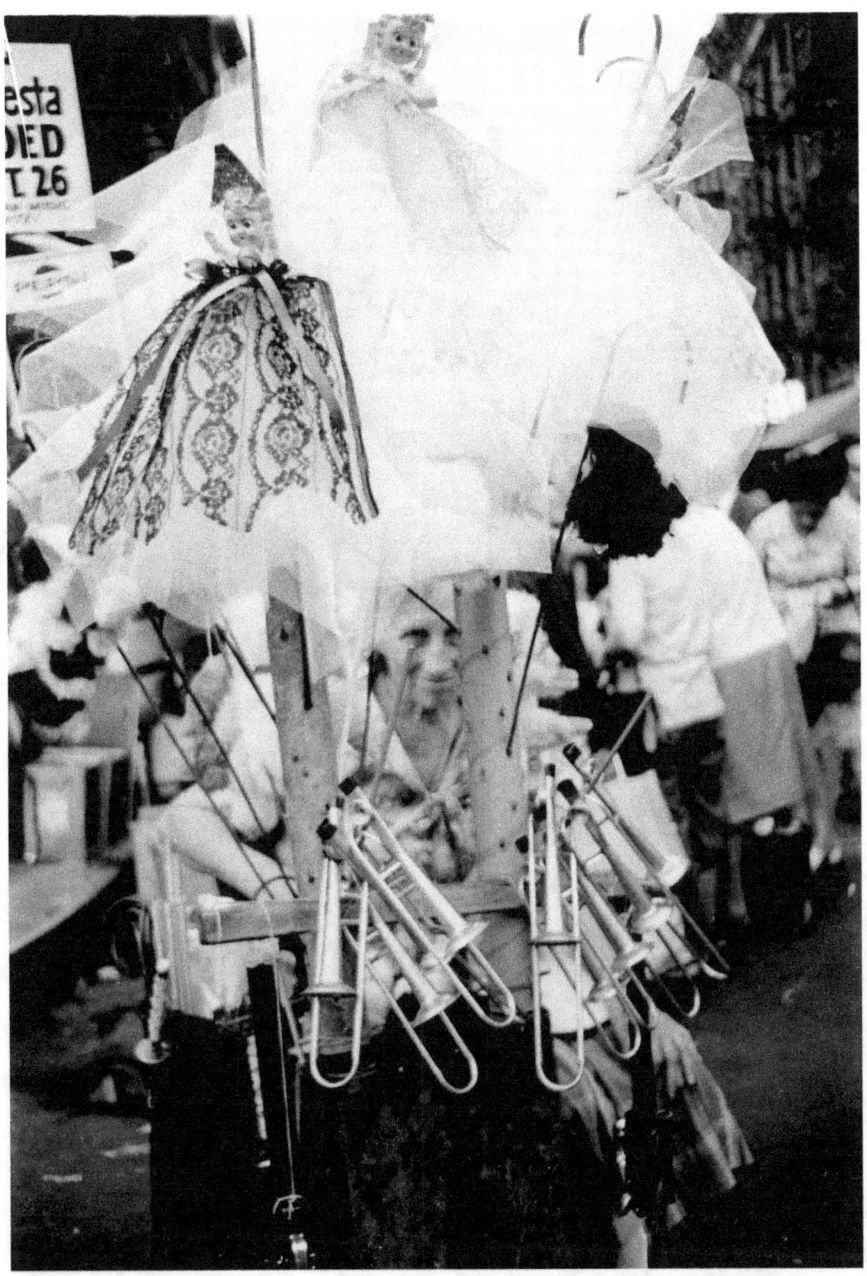

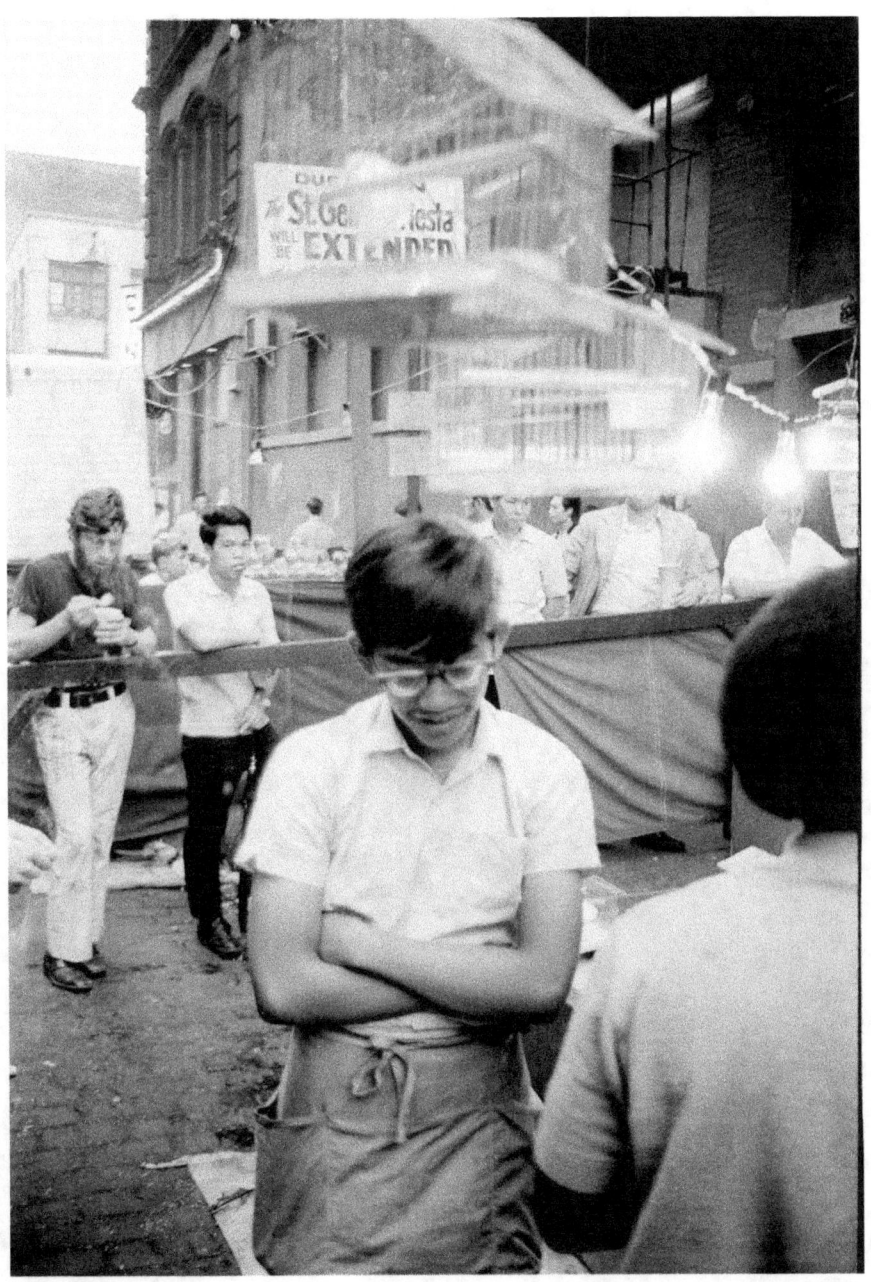

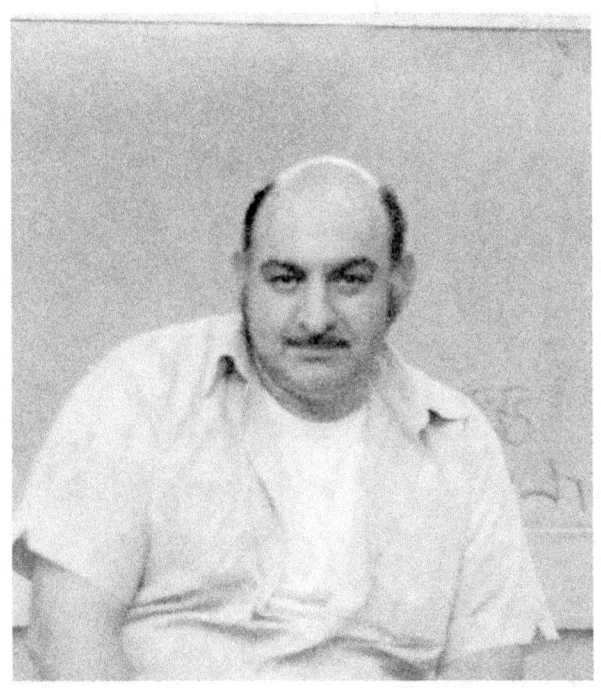

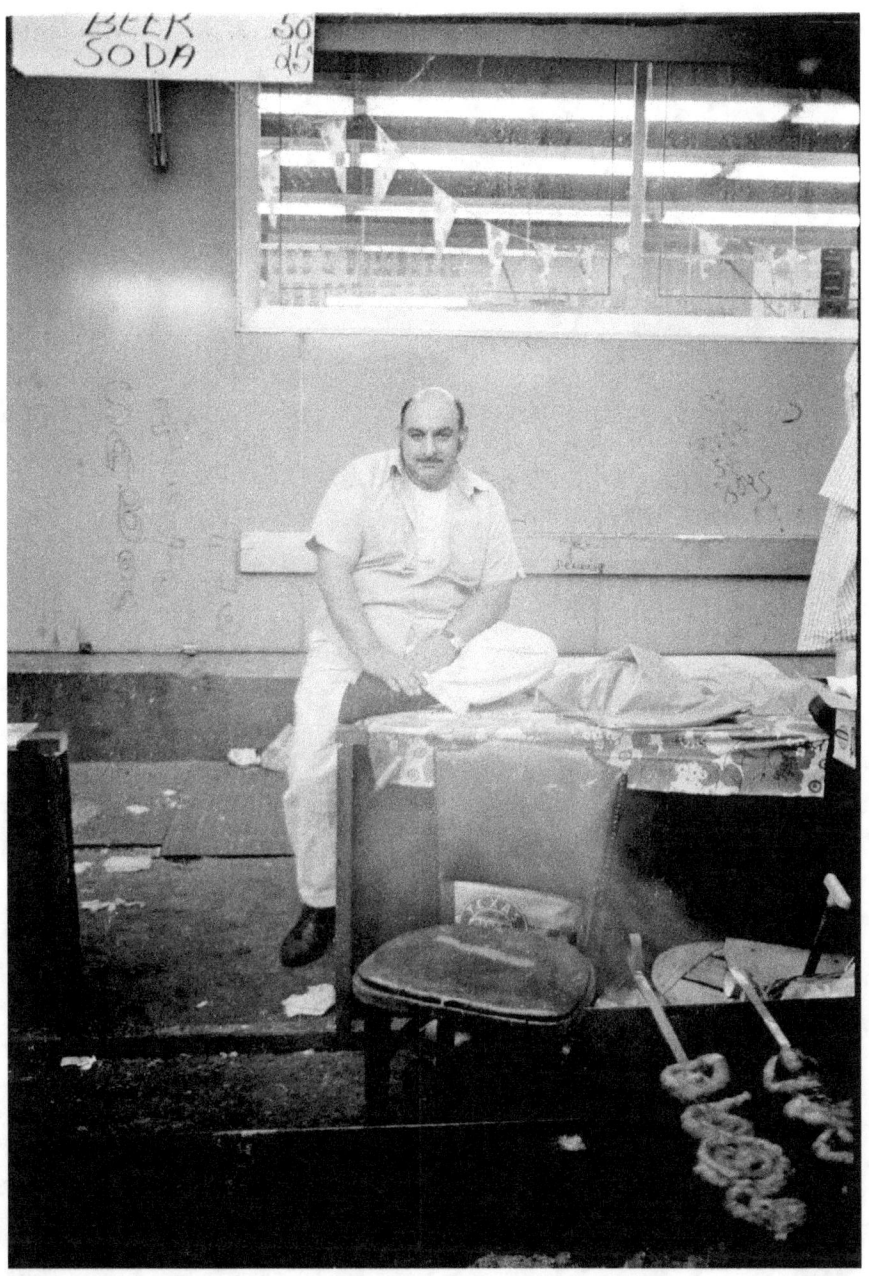

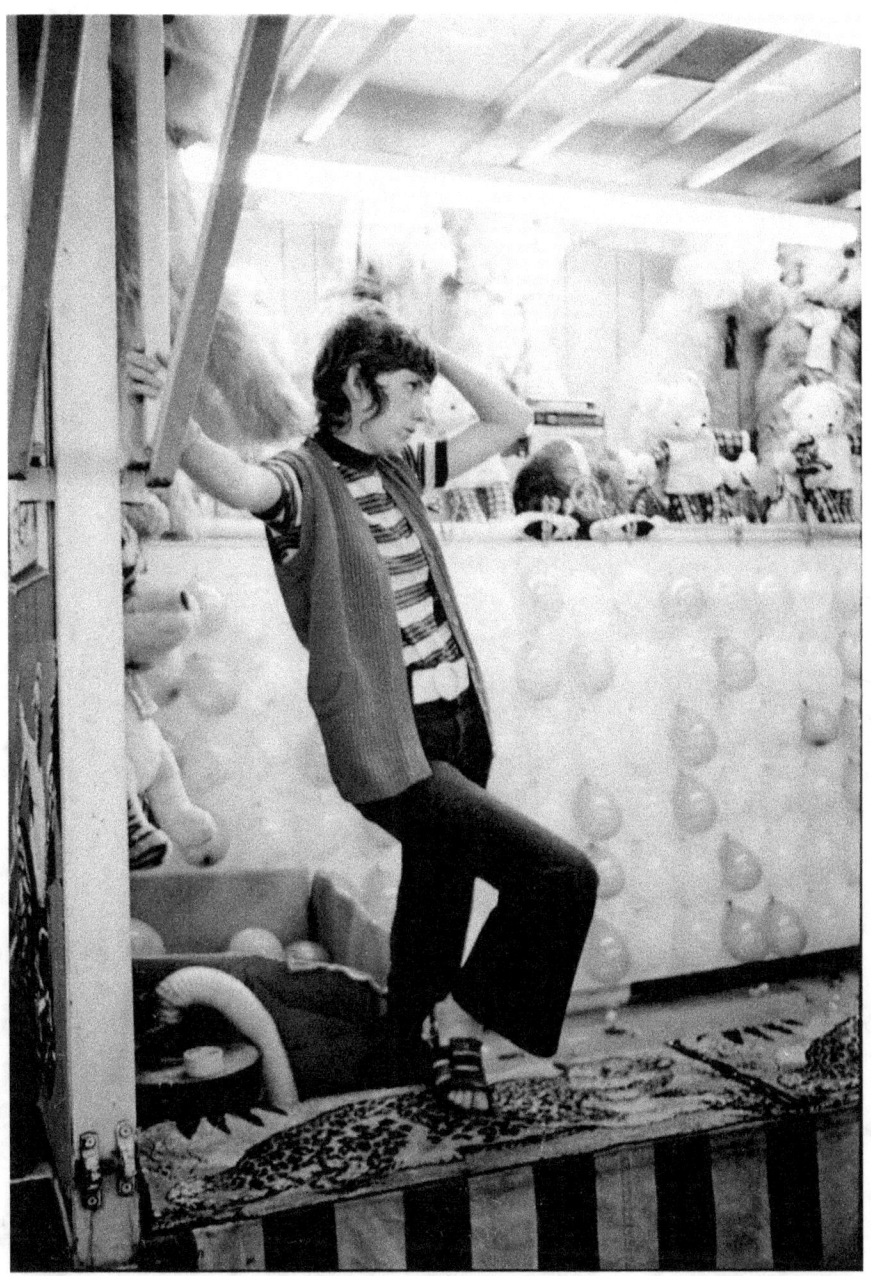

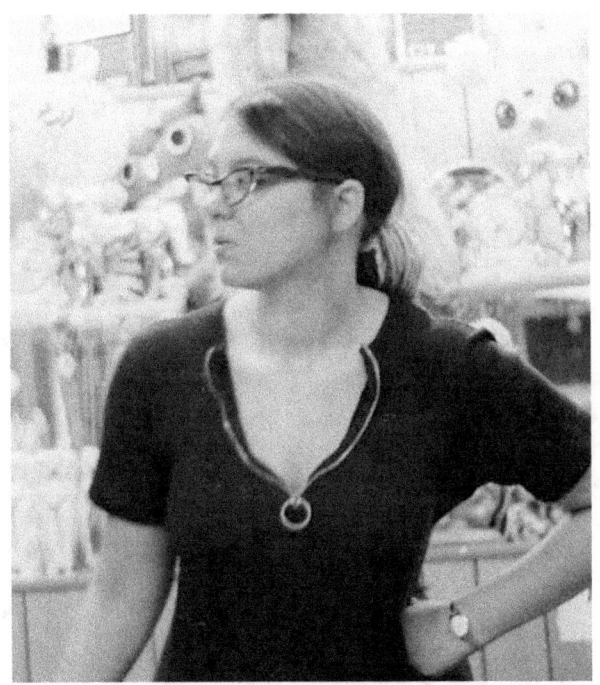

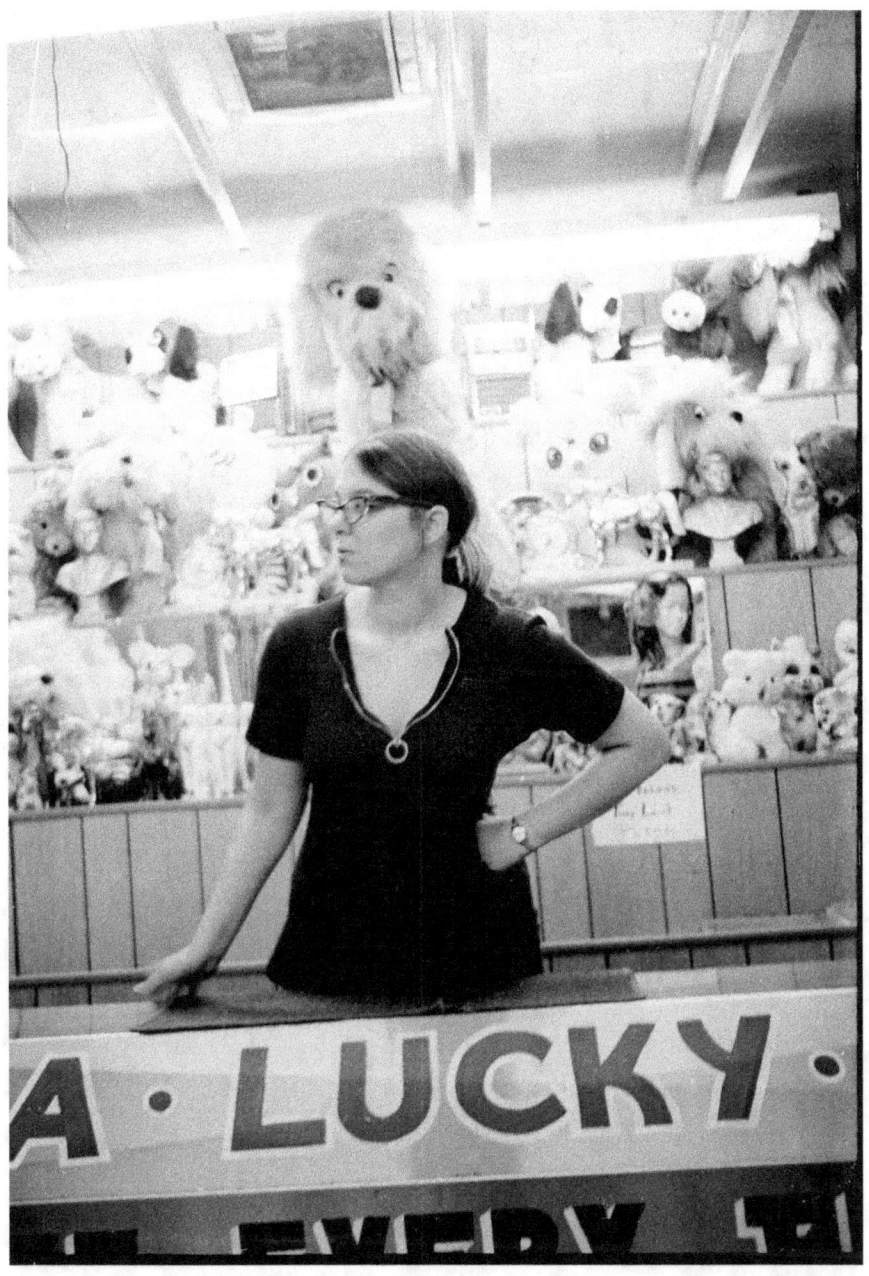

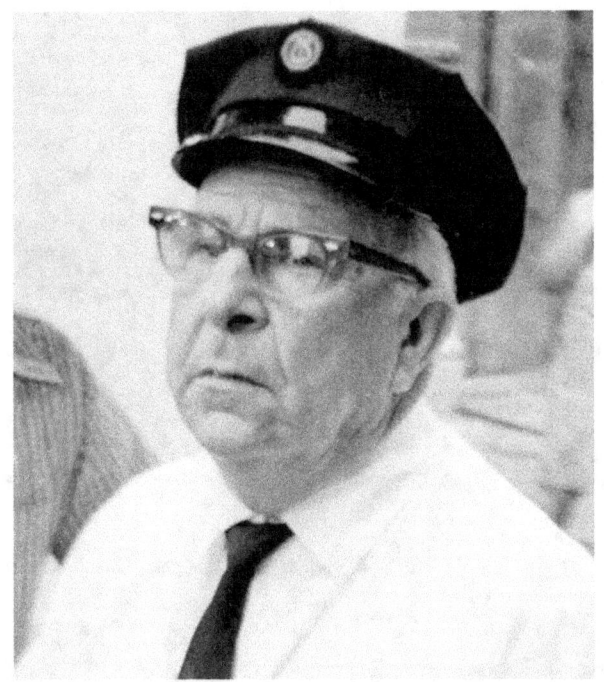

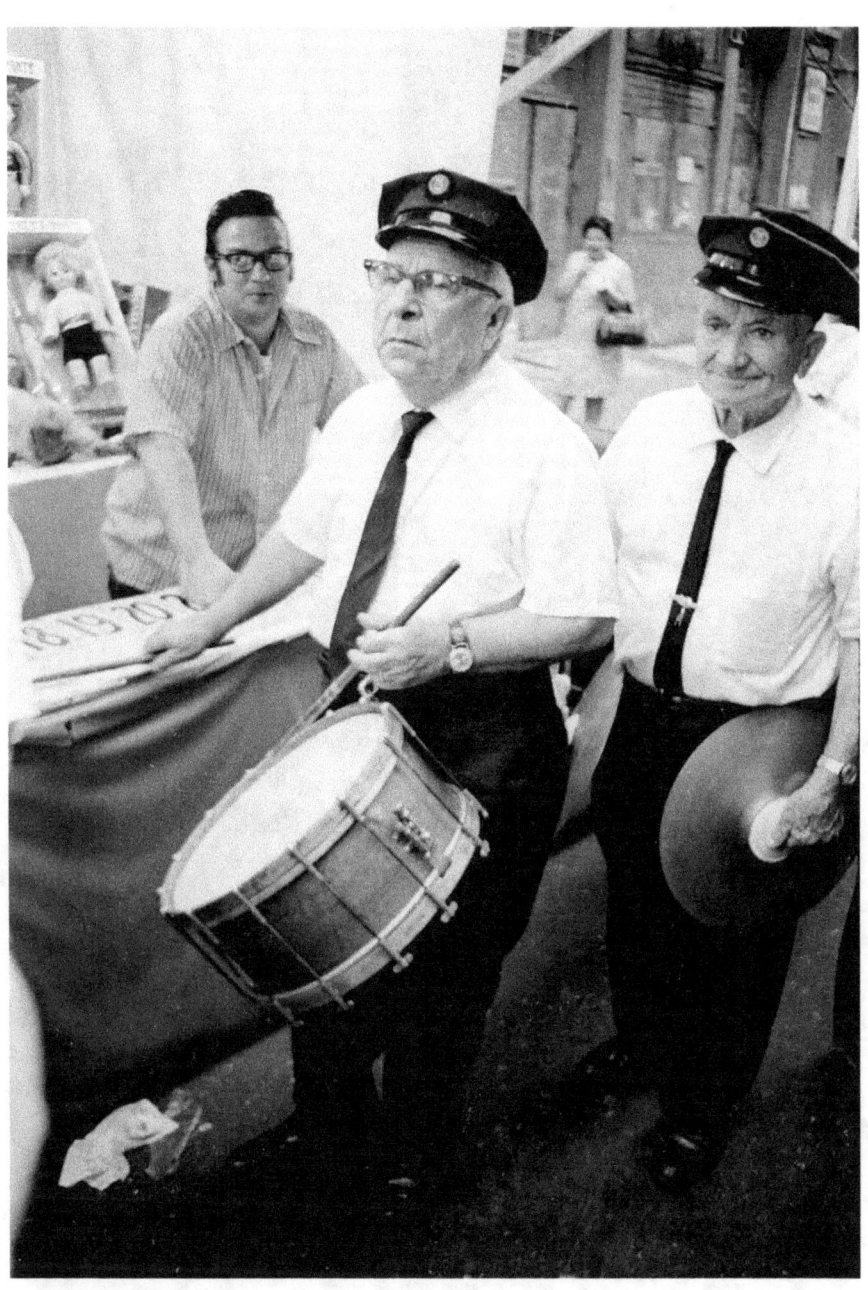

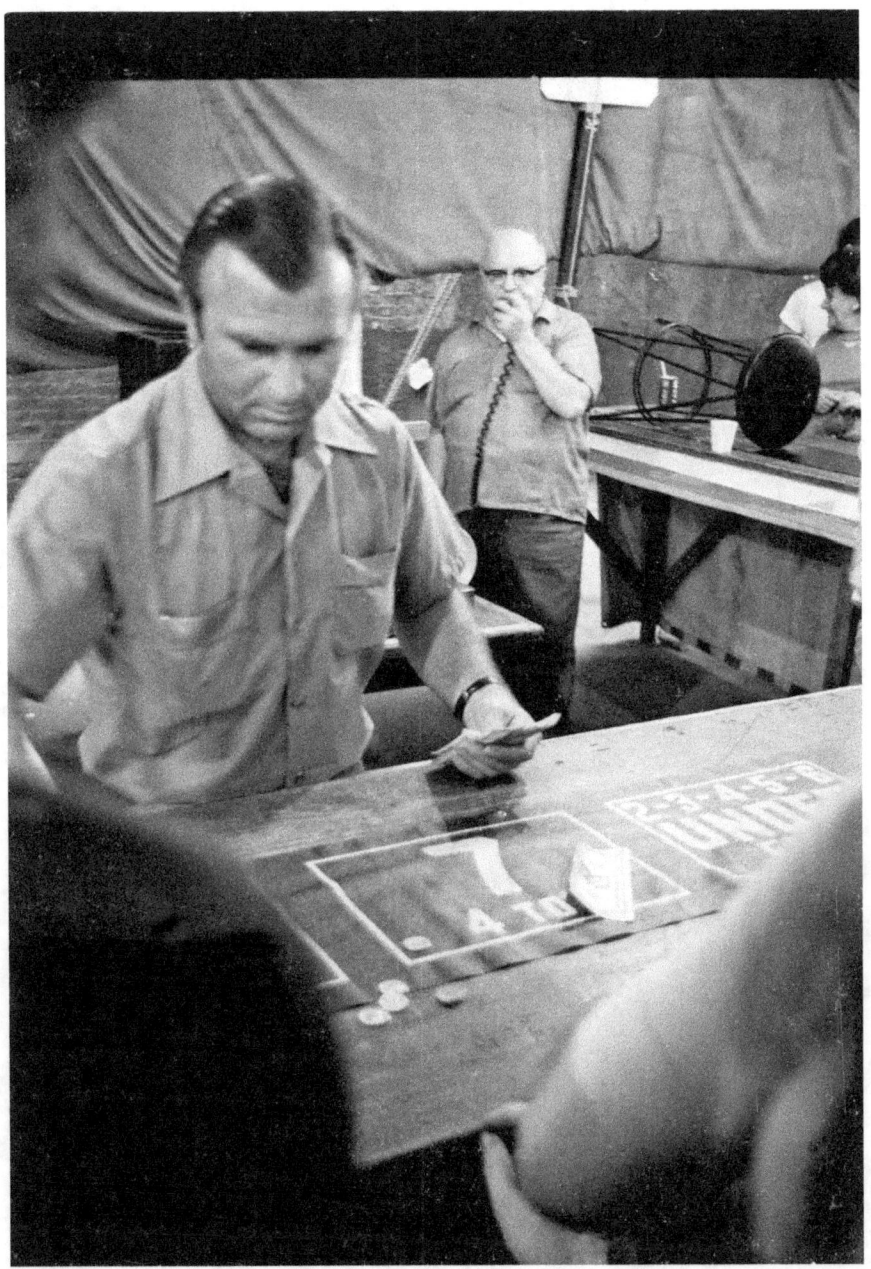

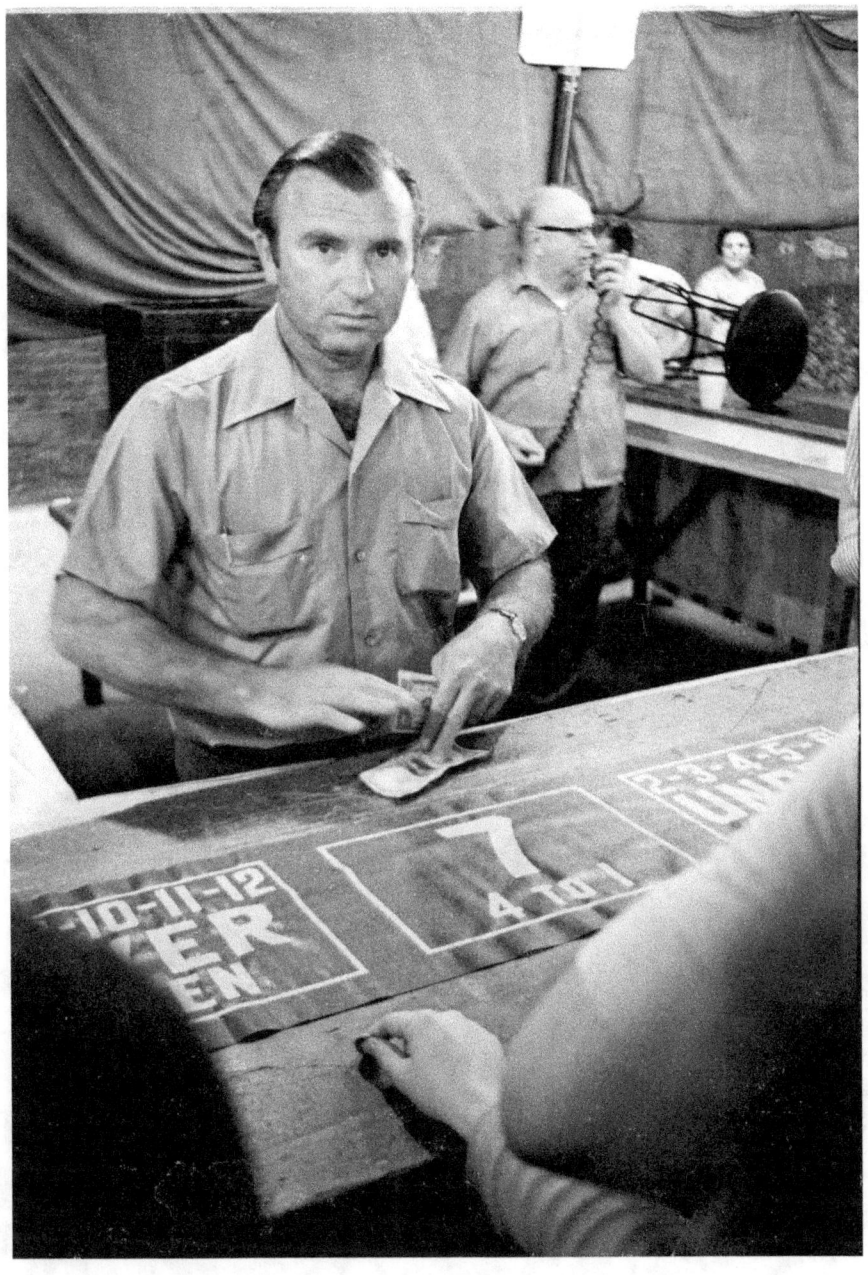

1971, The Food

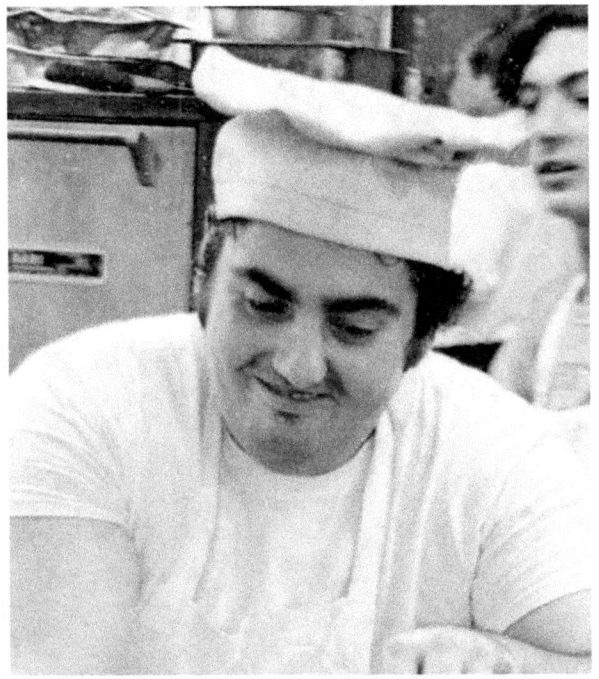

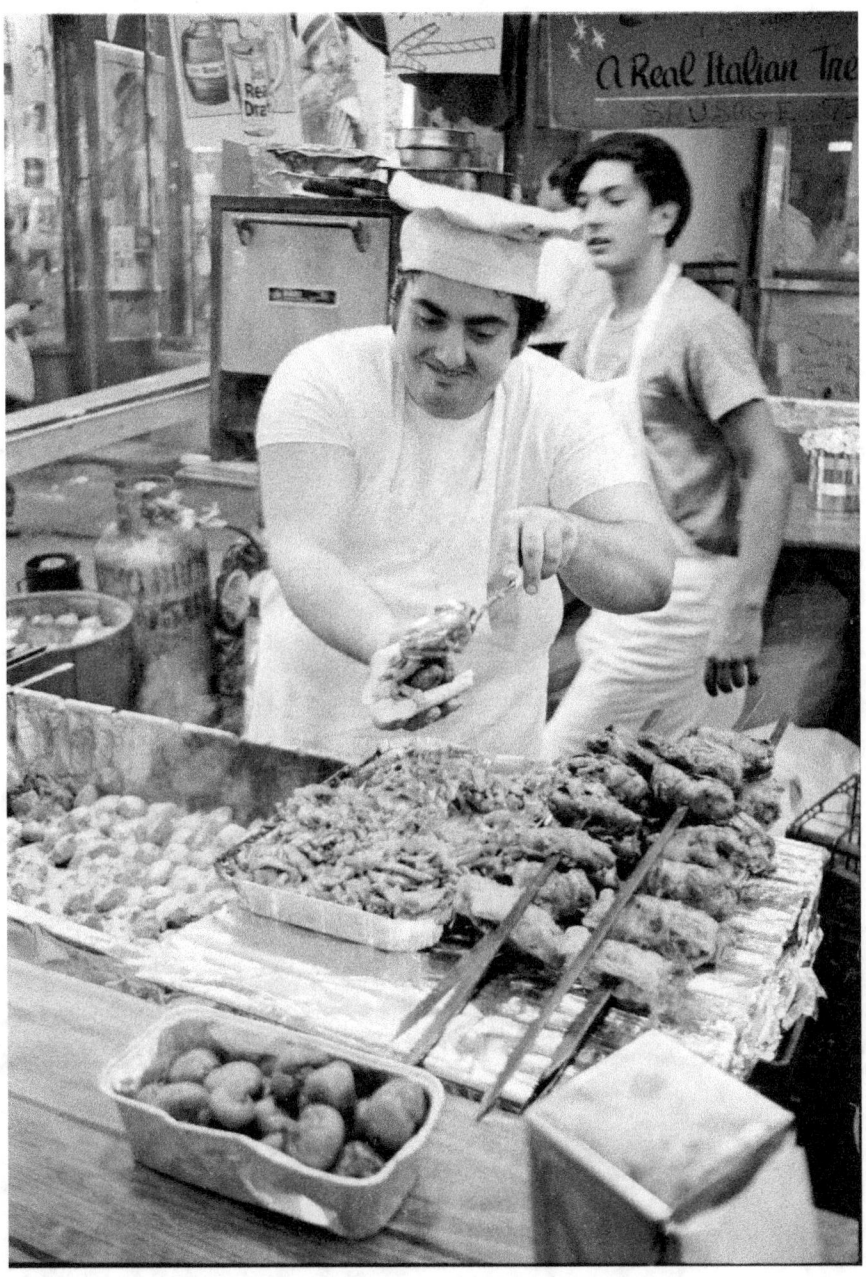

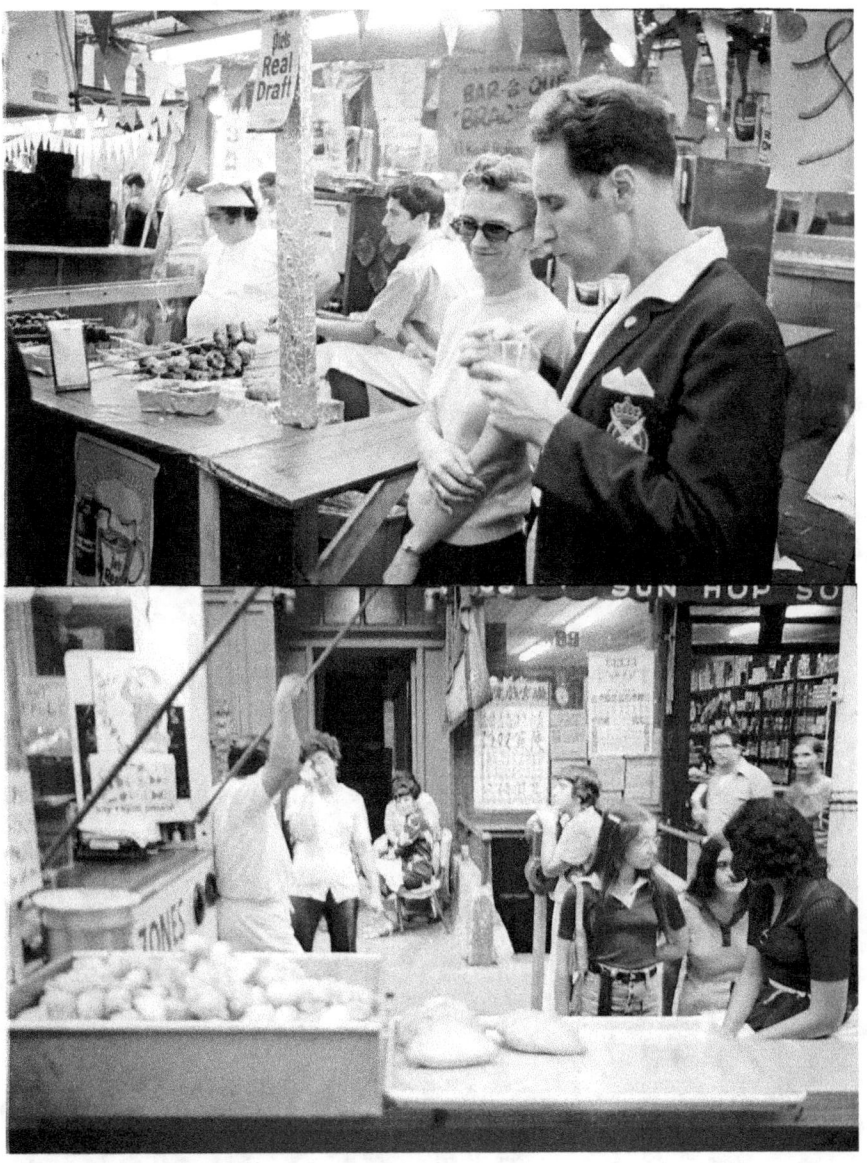

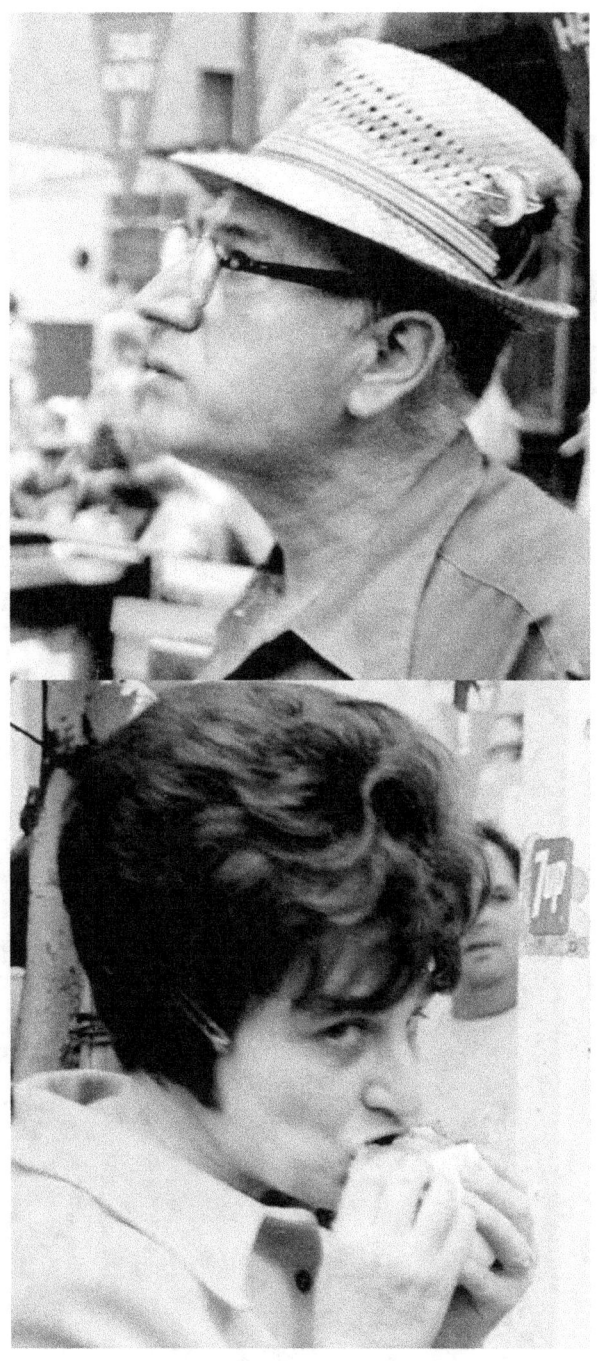

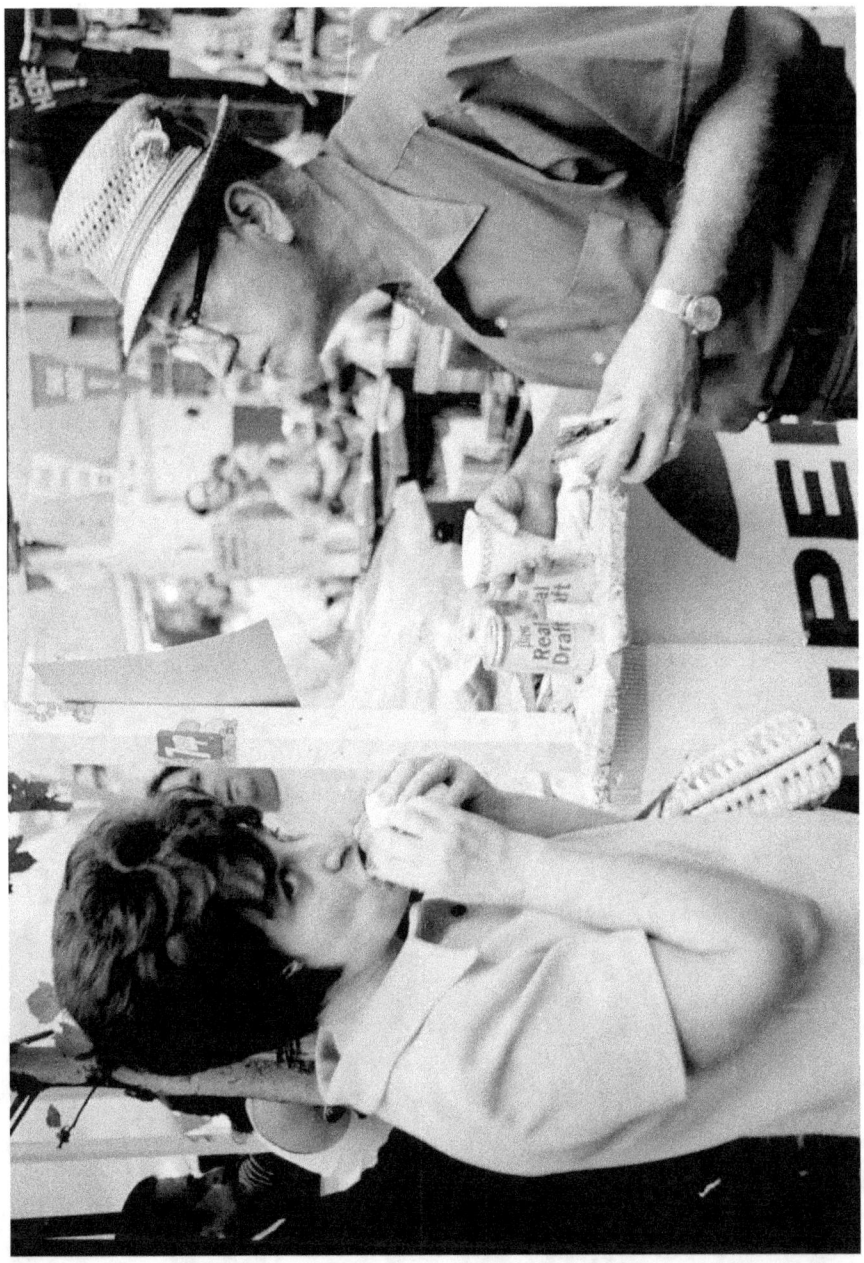

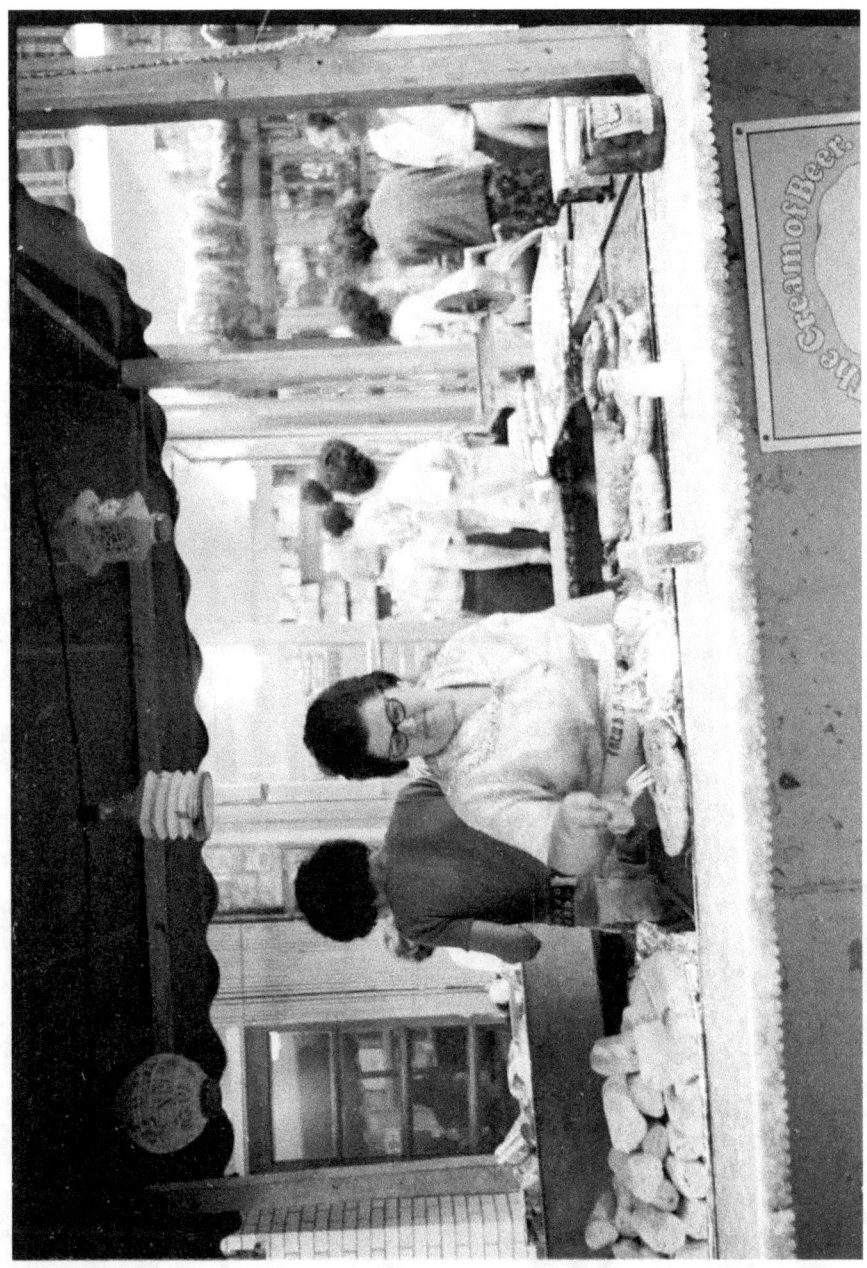

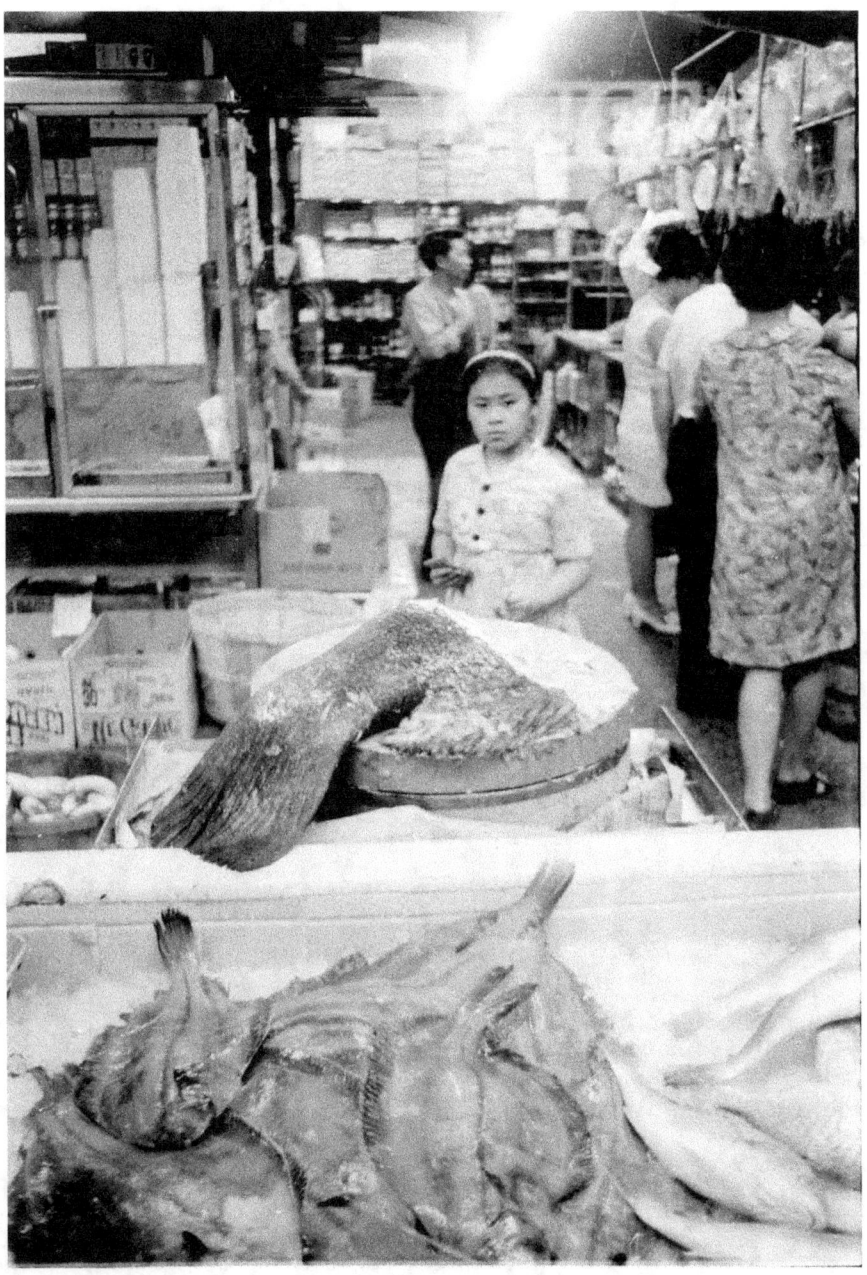

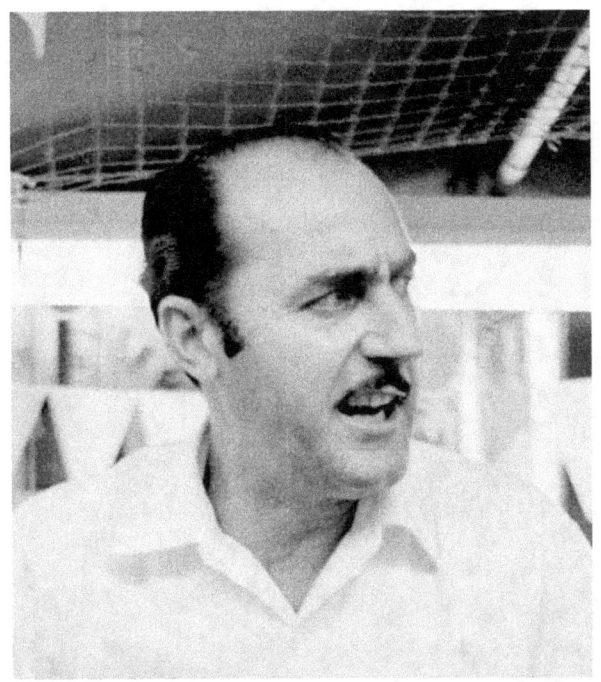

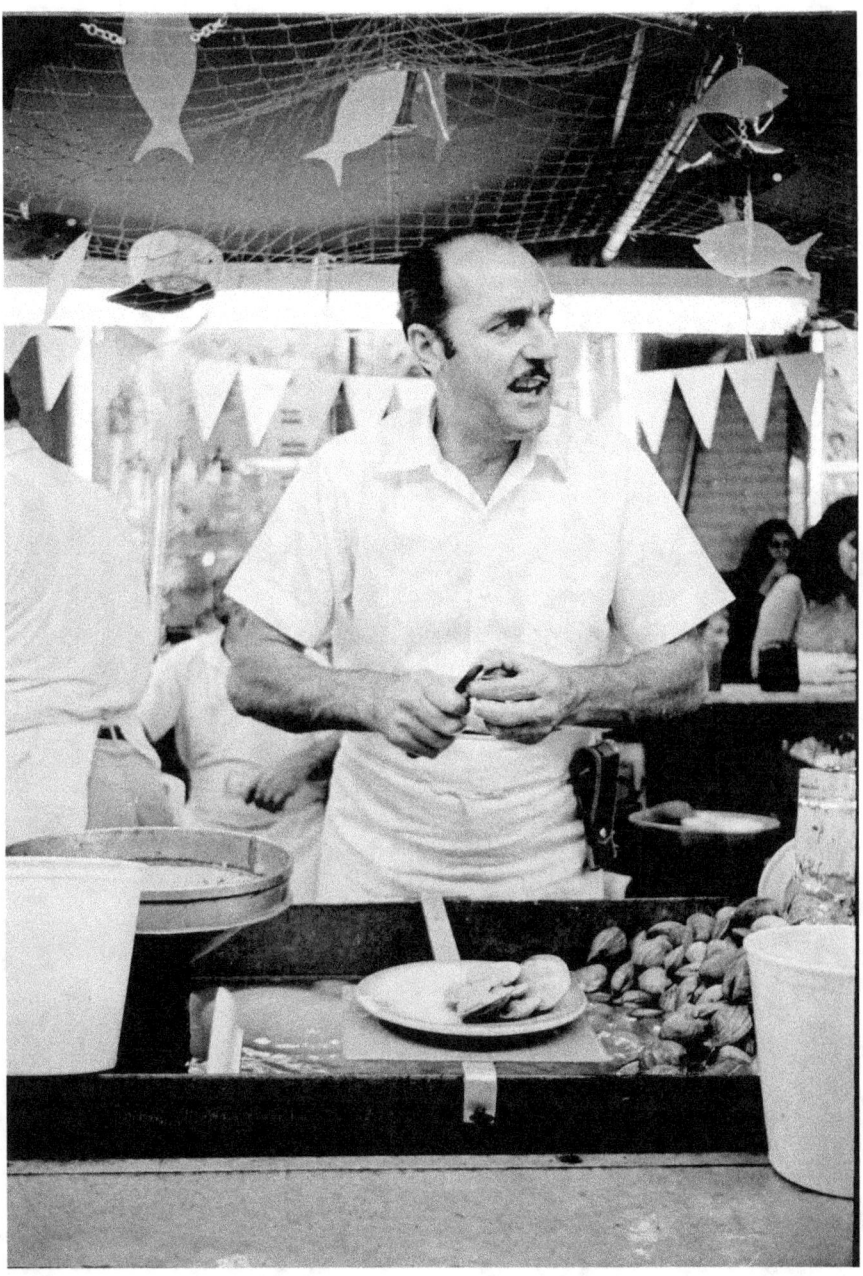

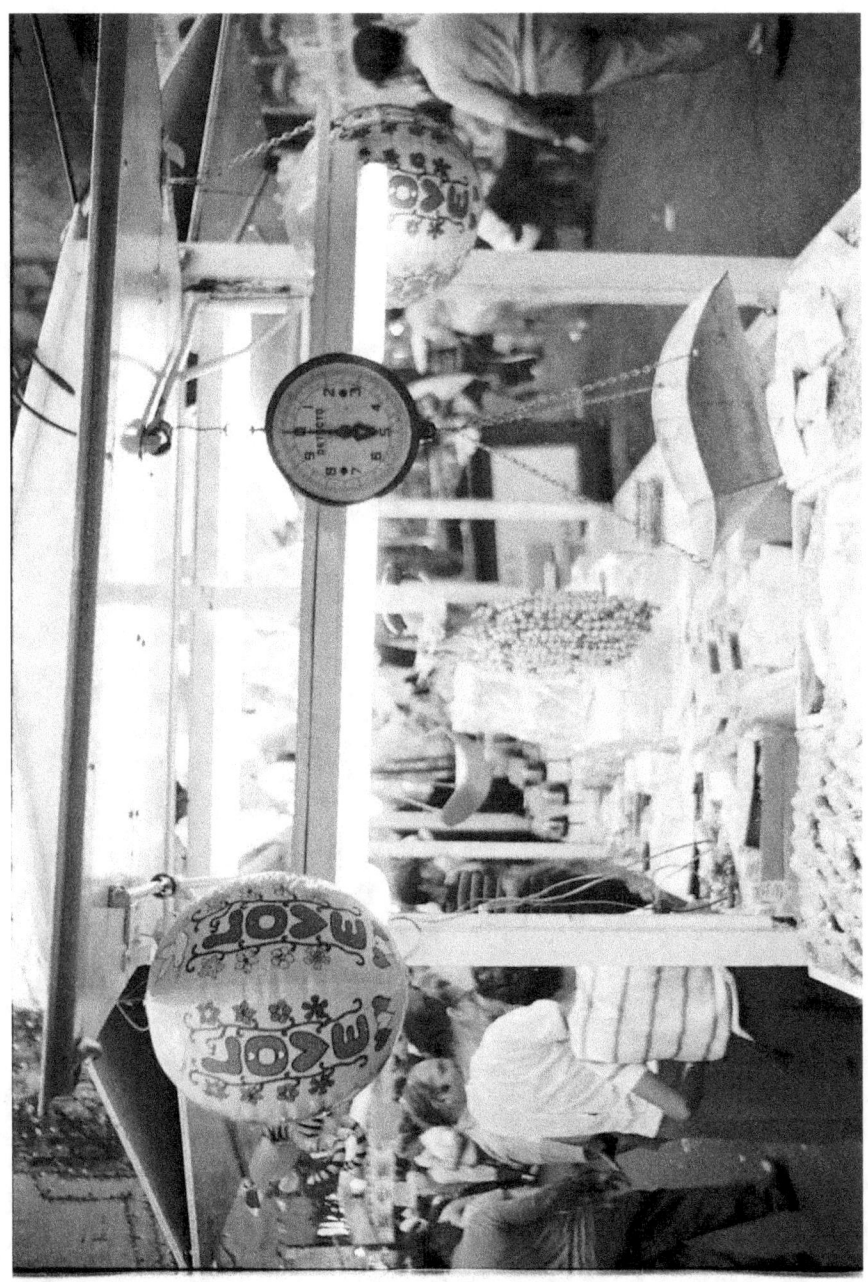

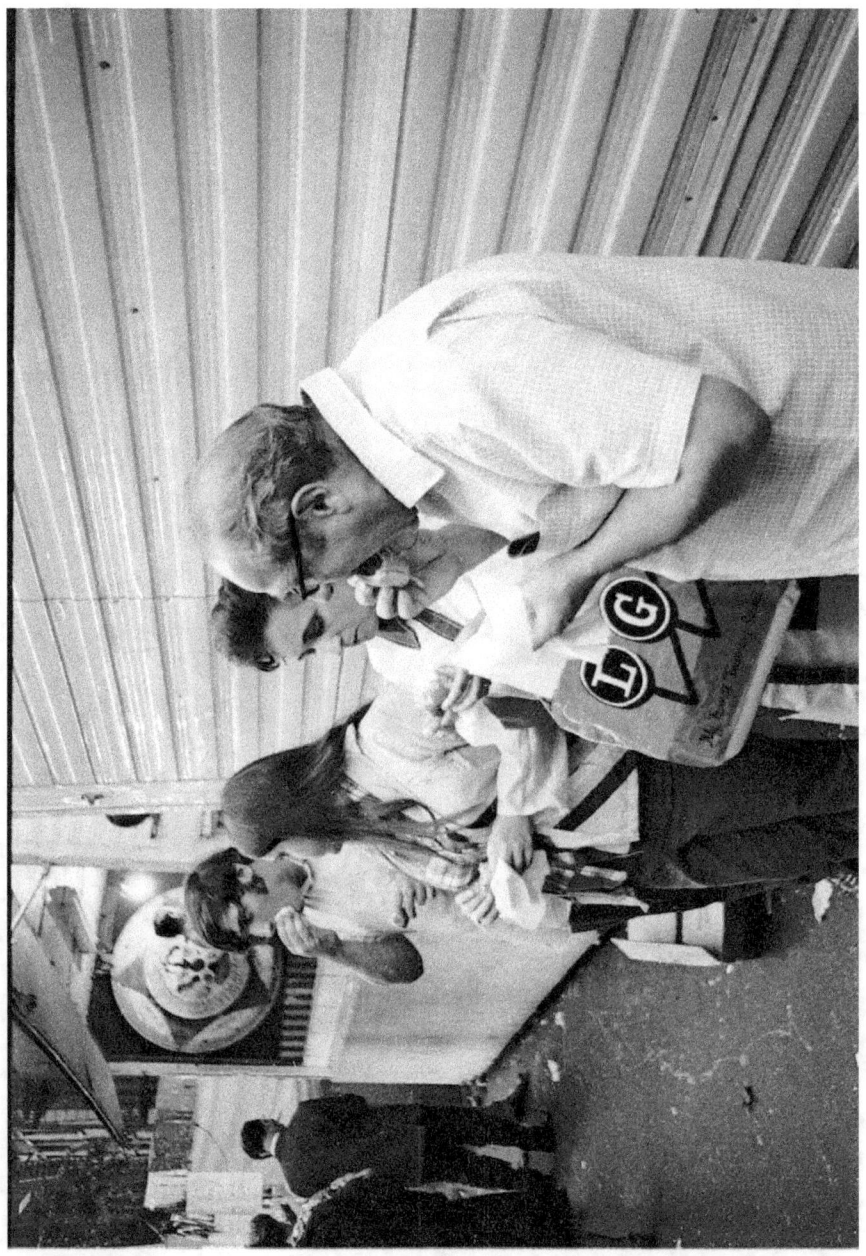

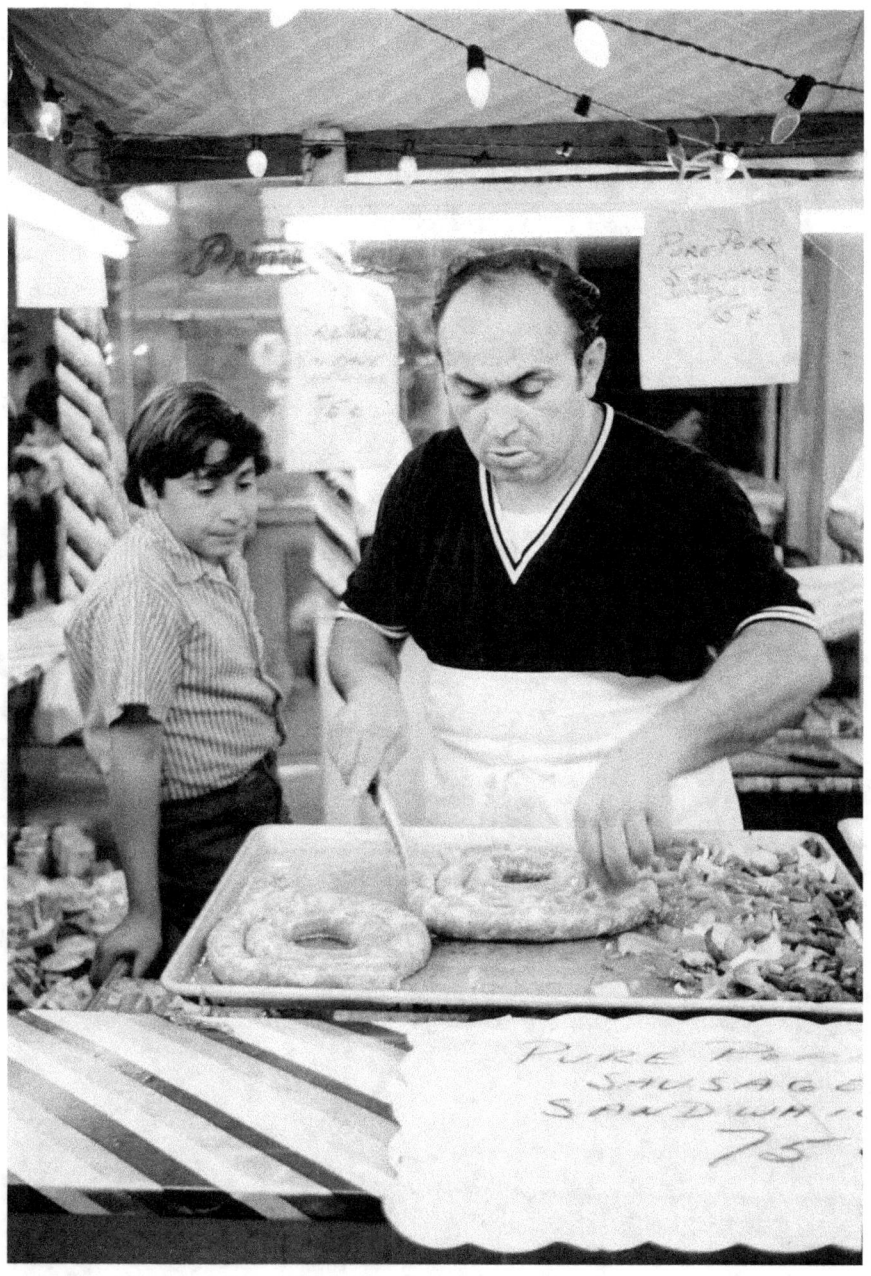

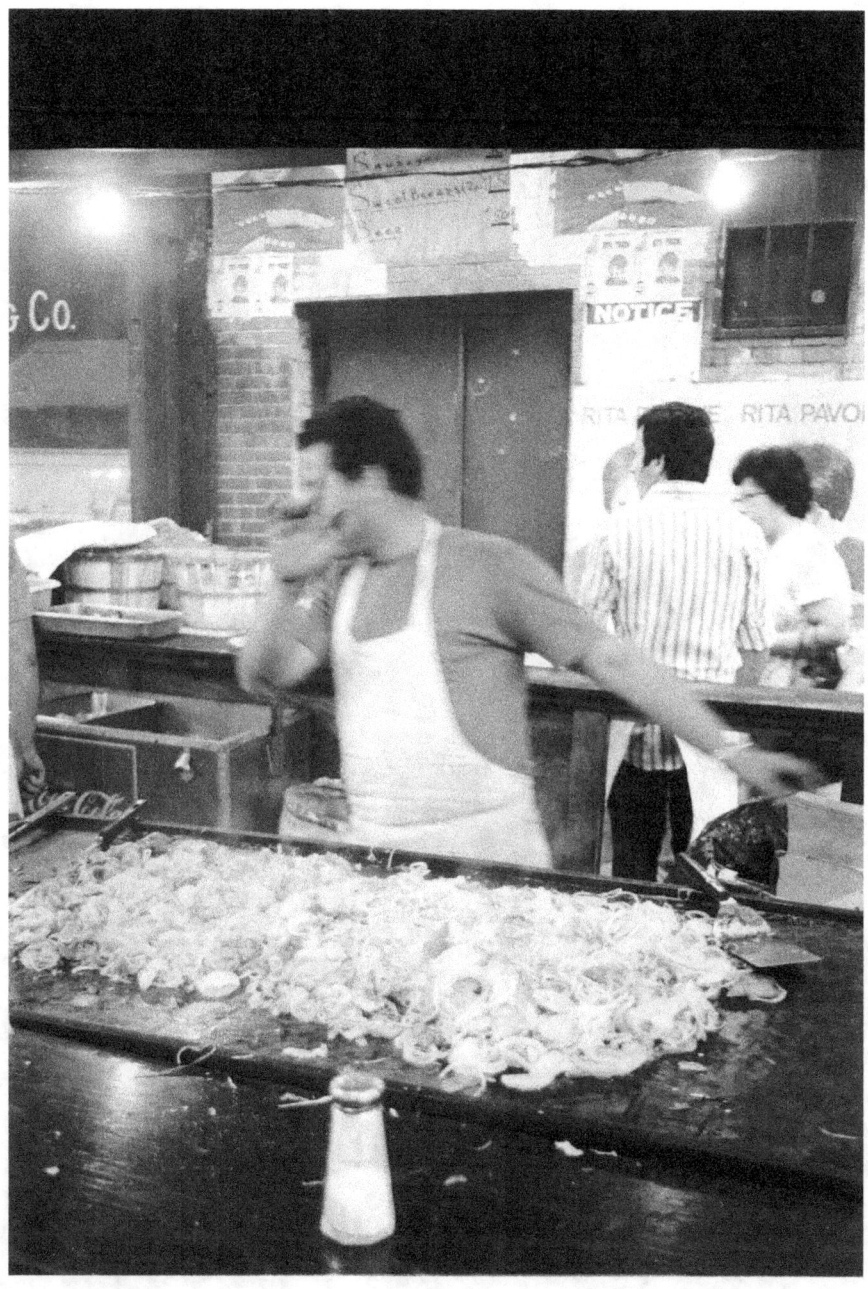

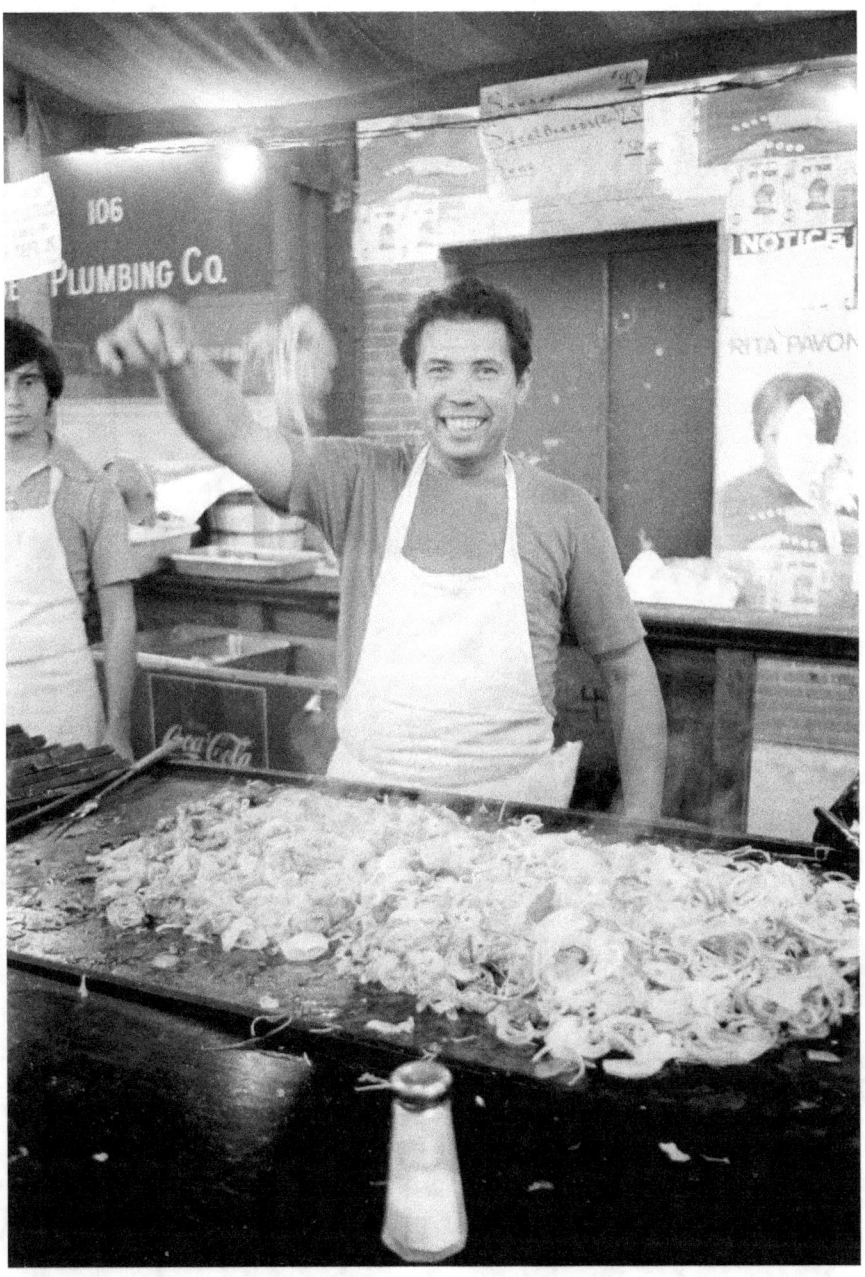

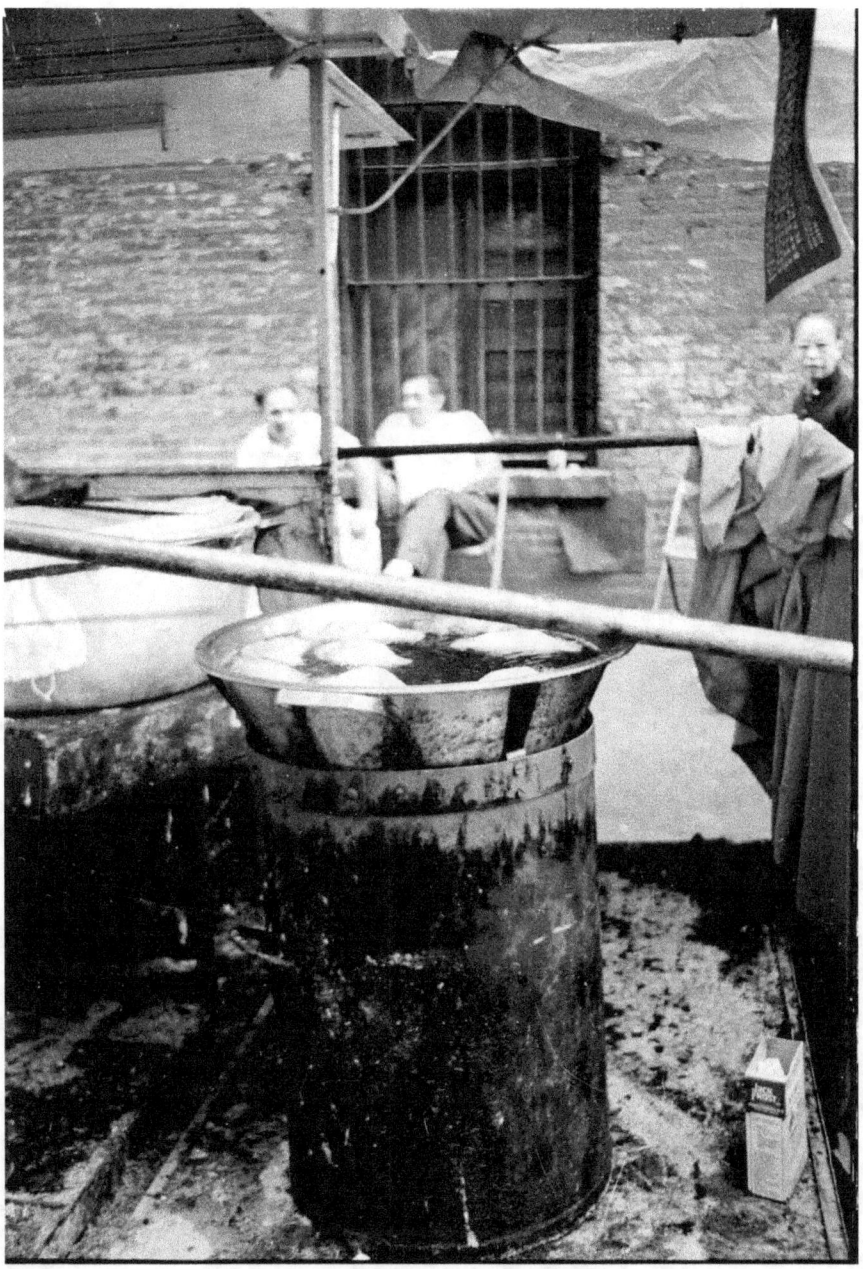

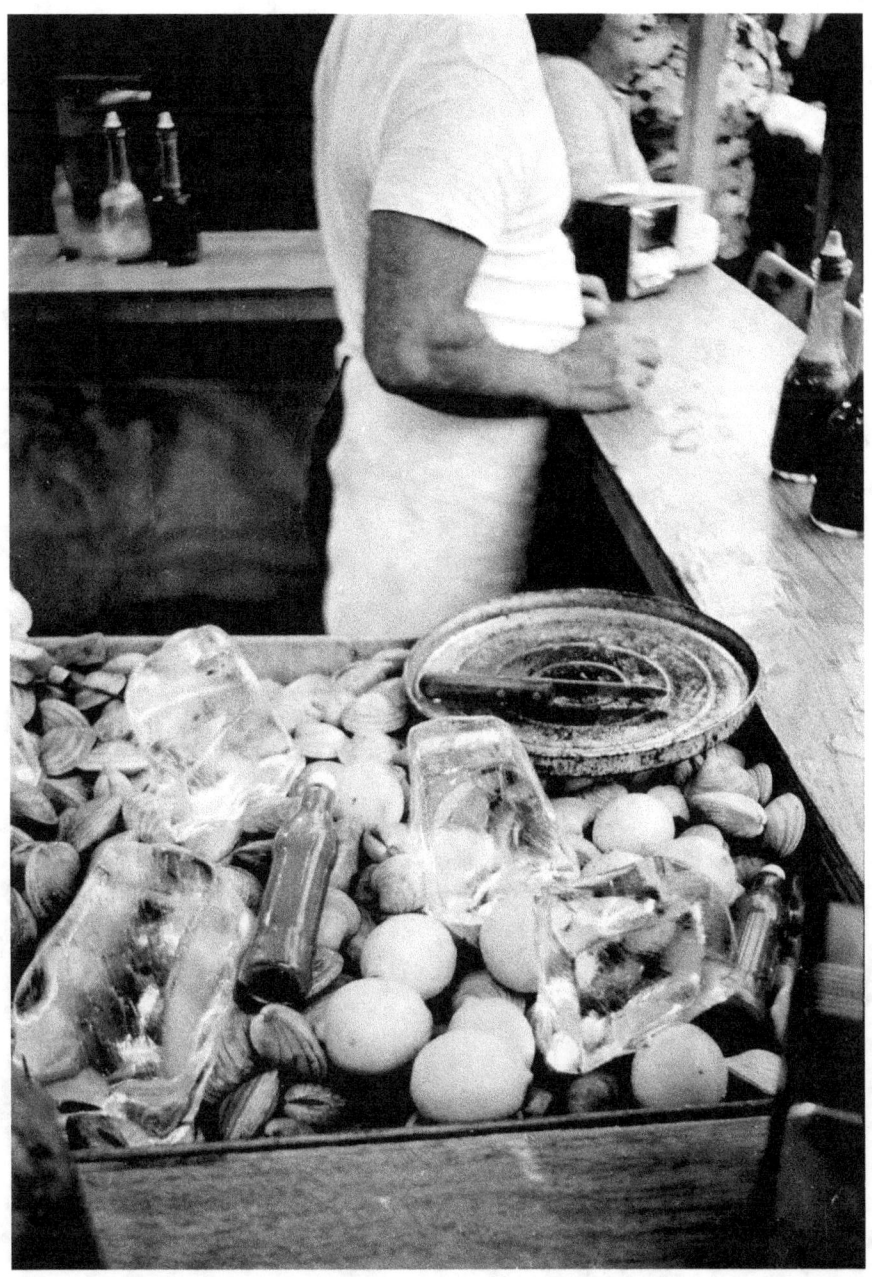

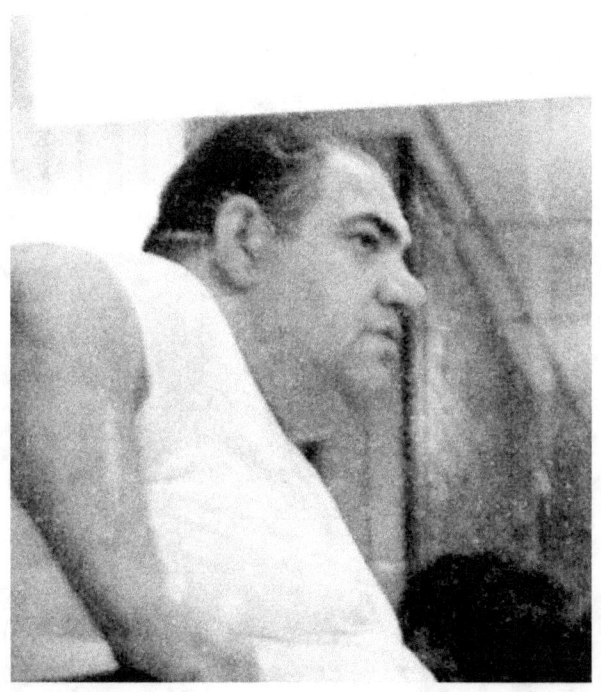

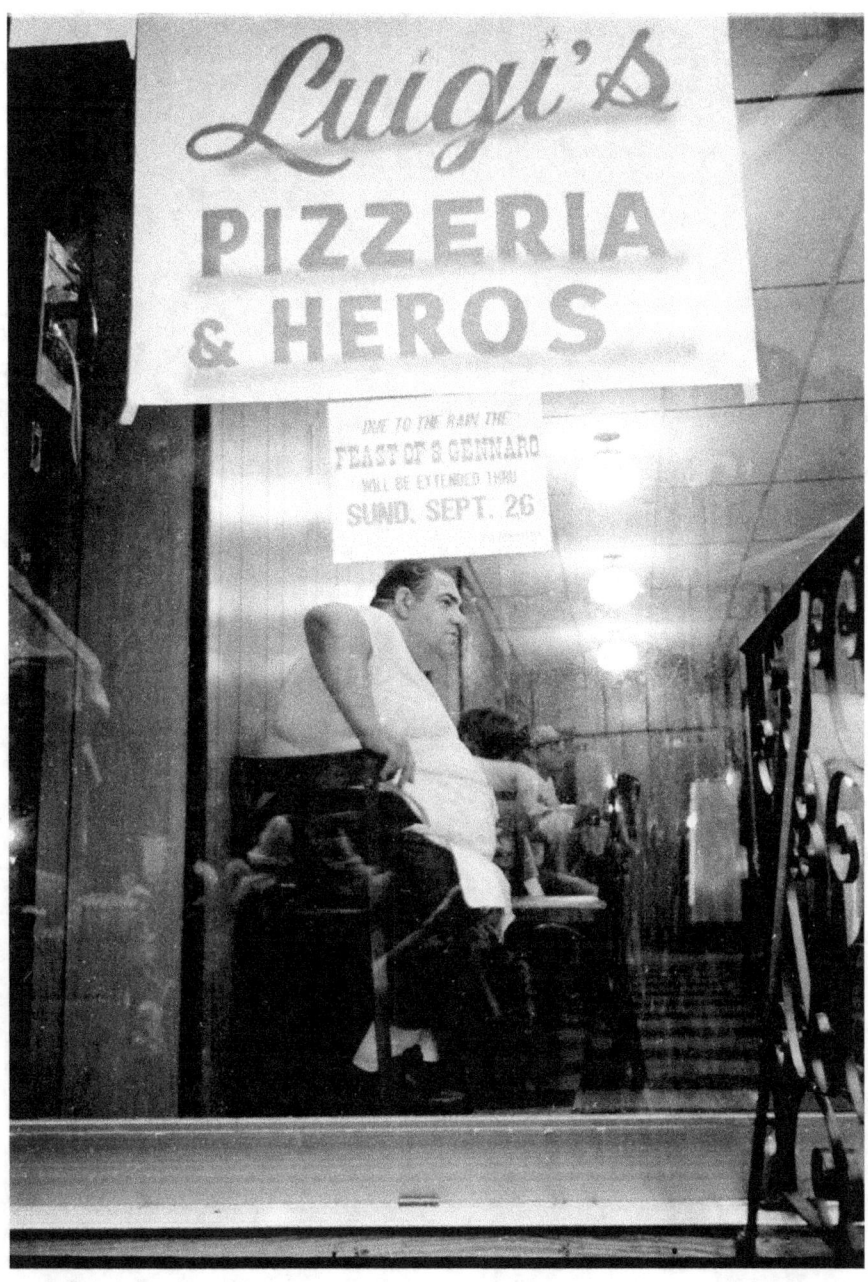

1971, Activities

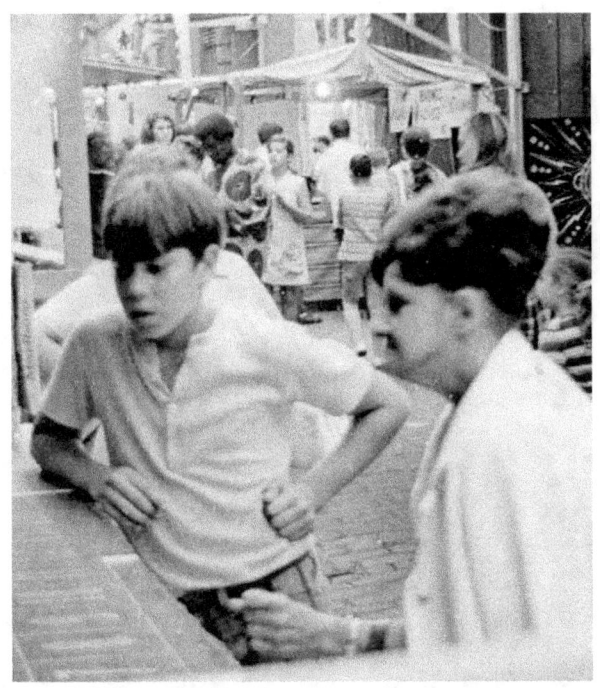

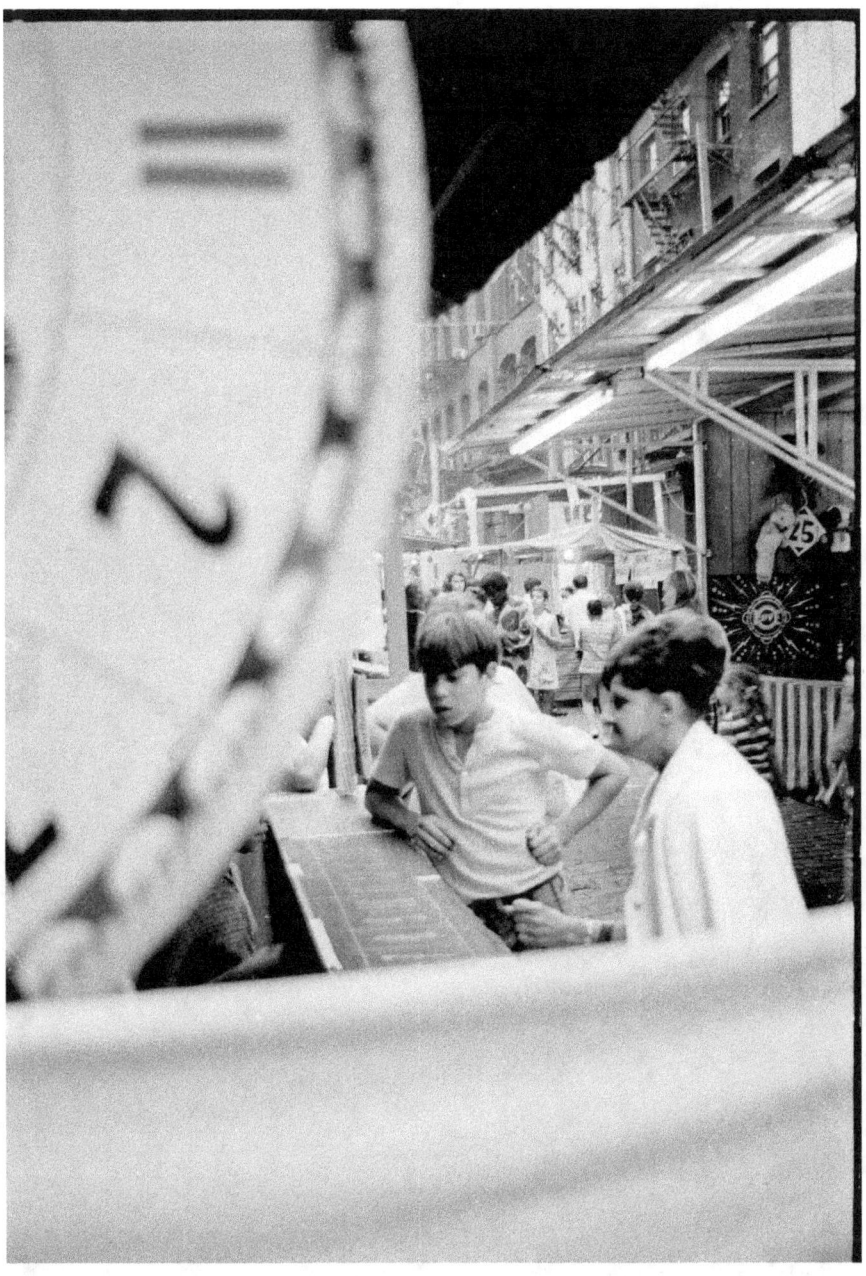

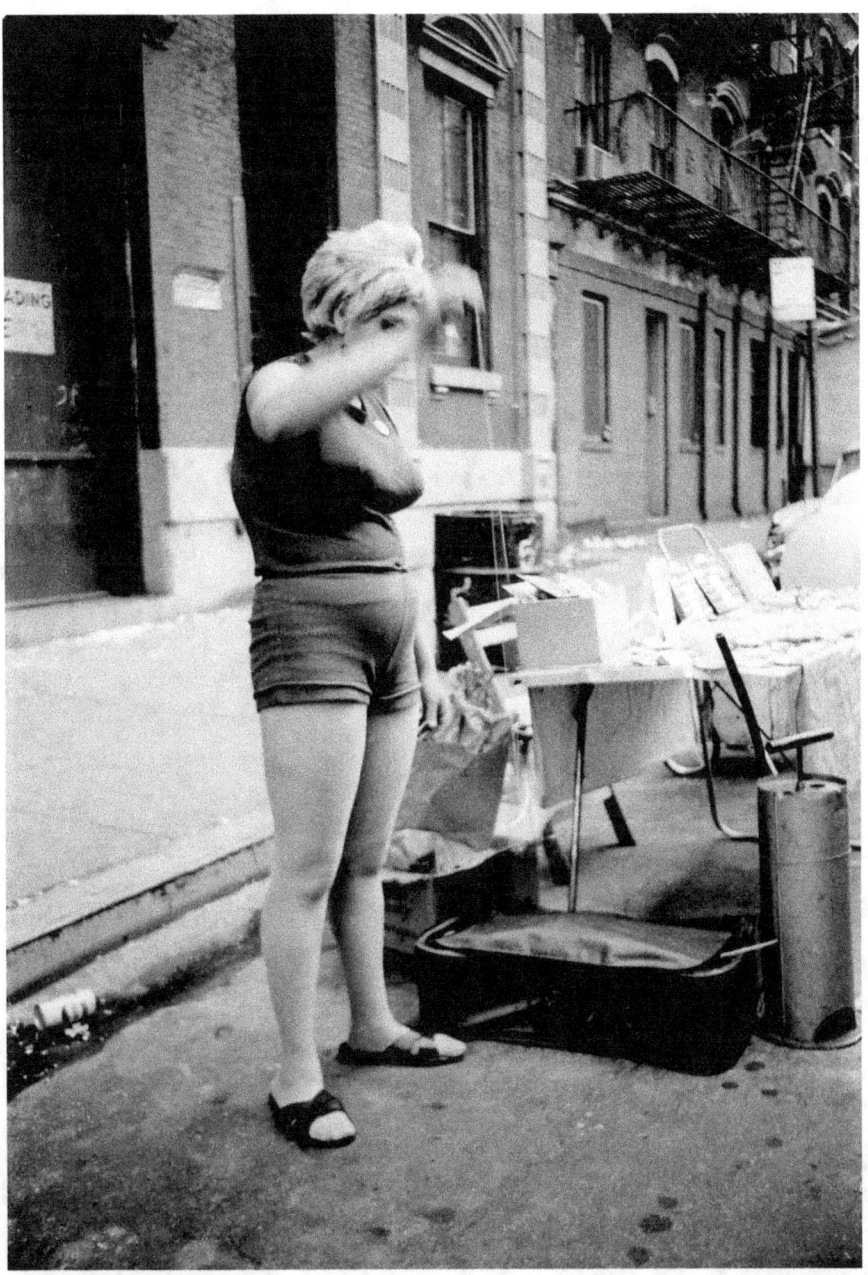

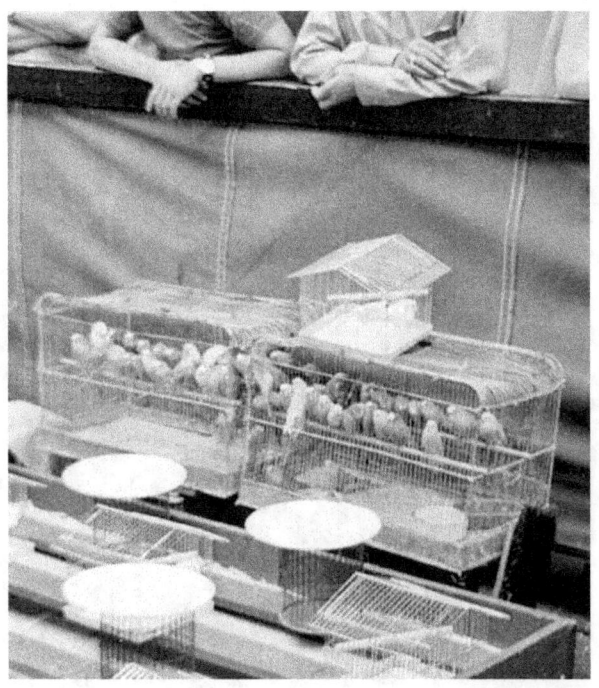

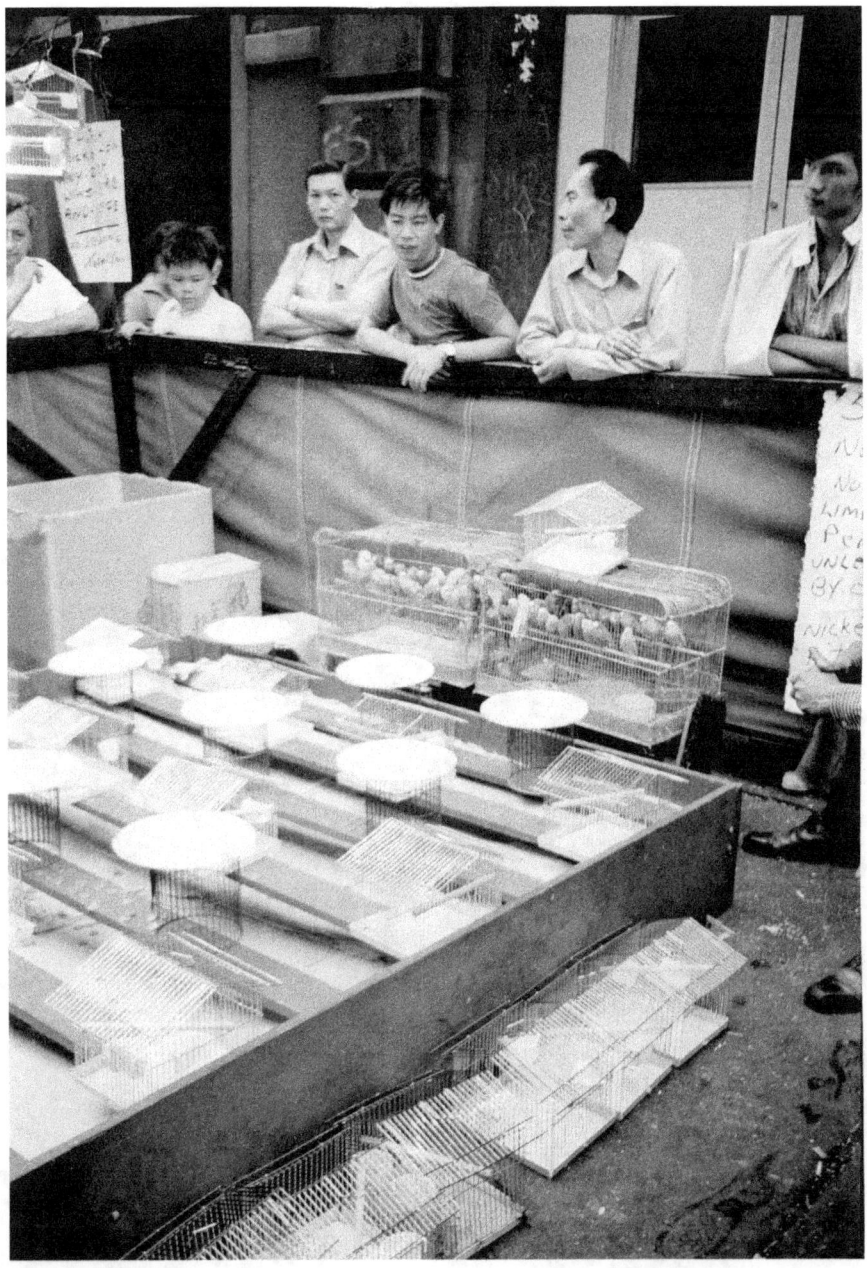

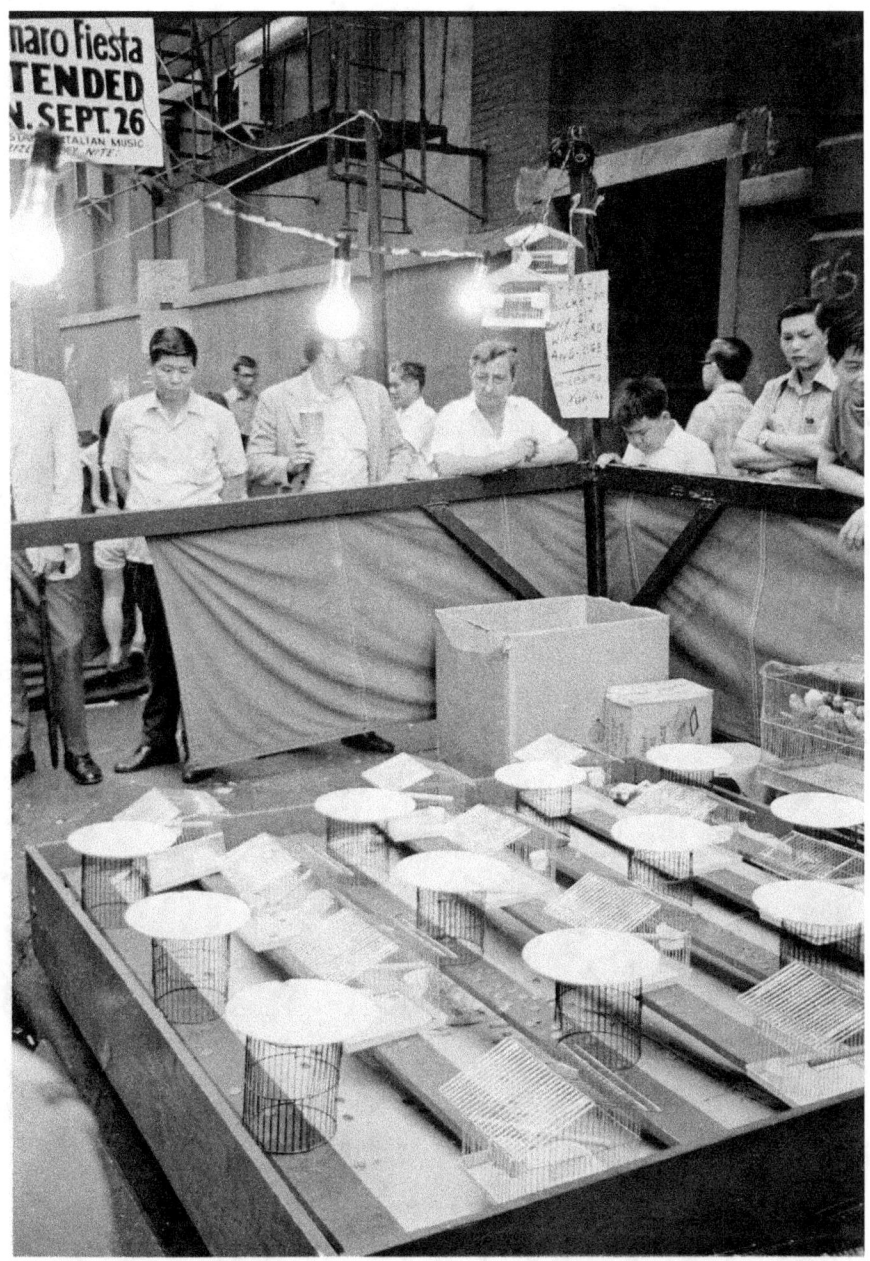

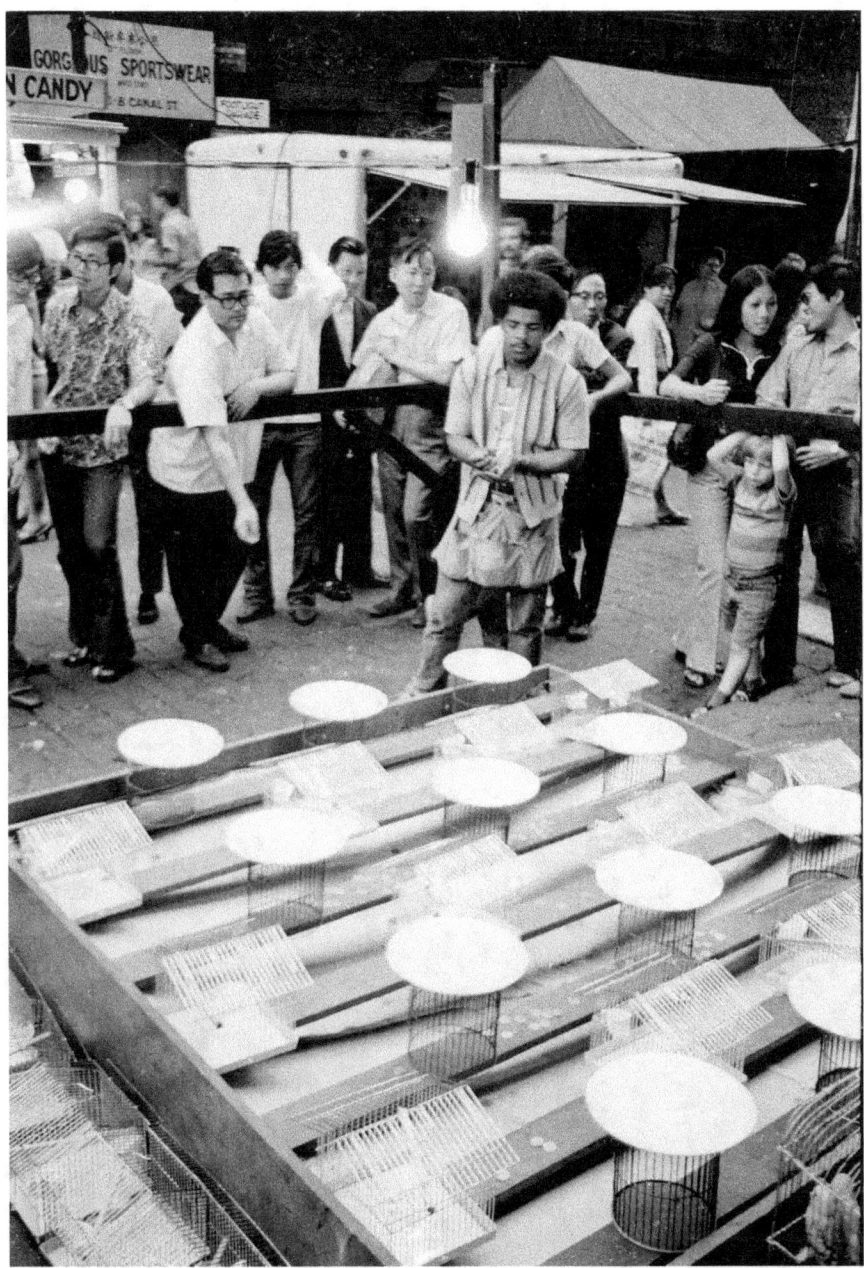

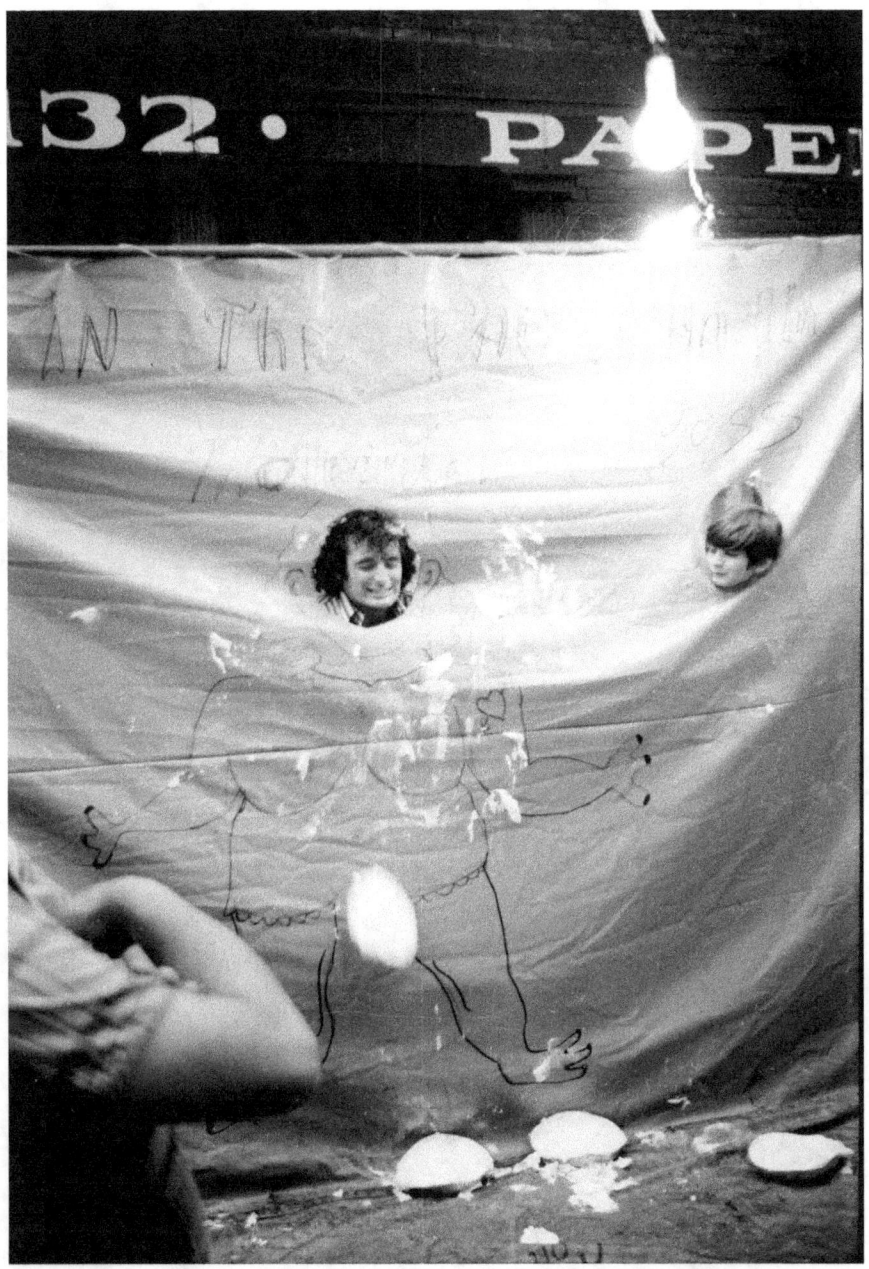

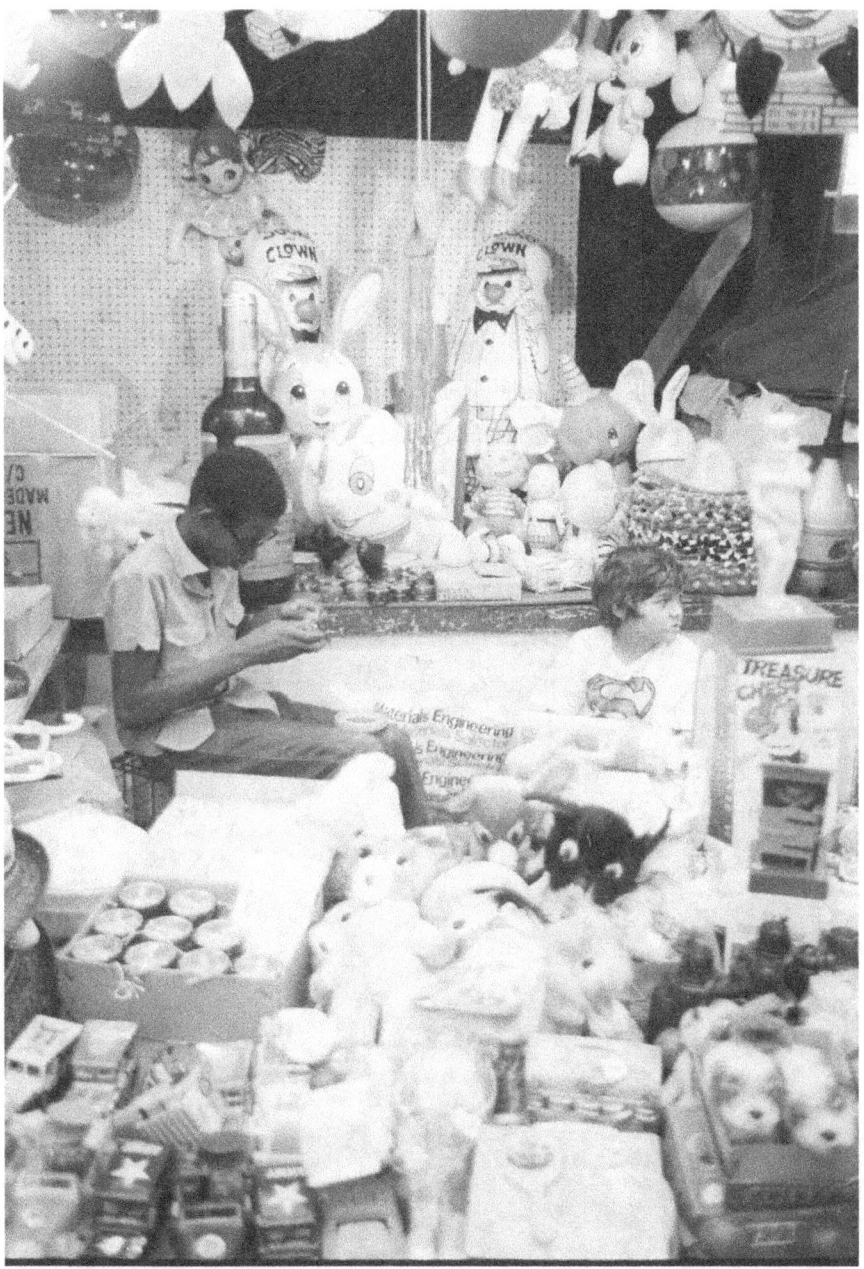

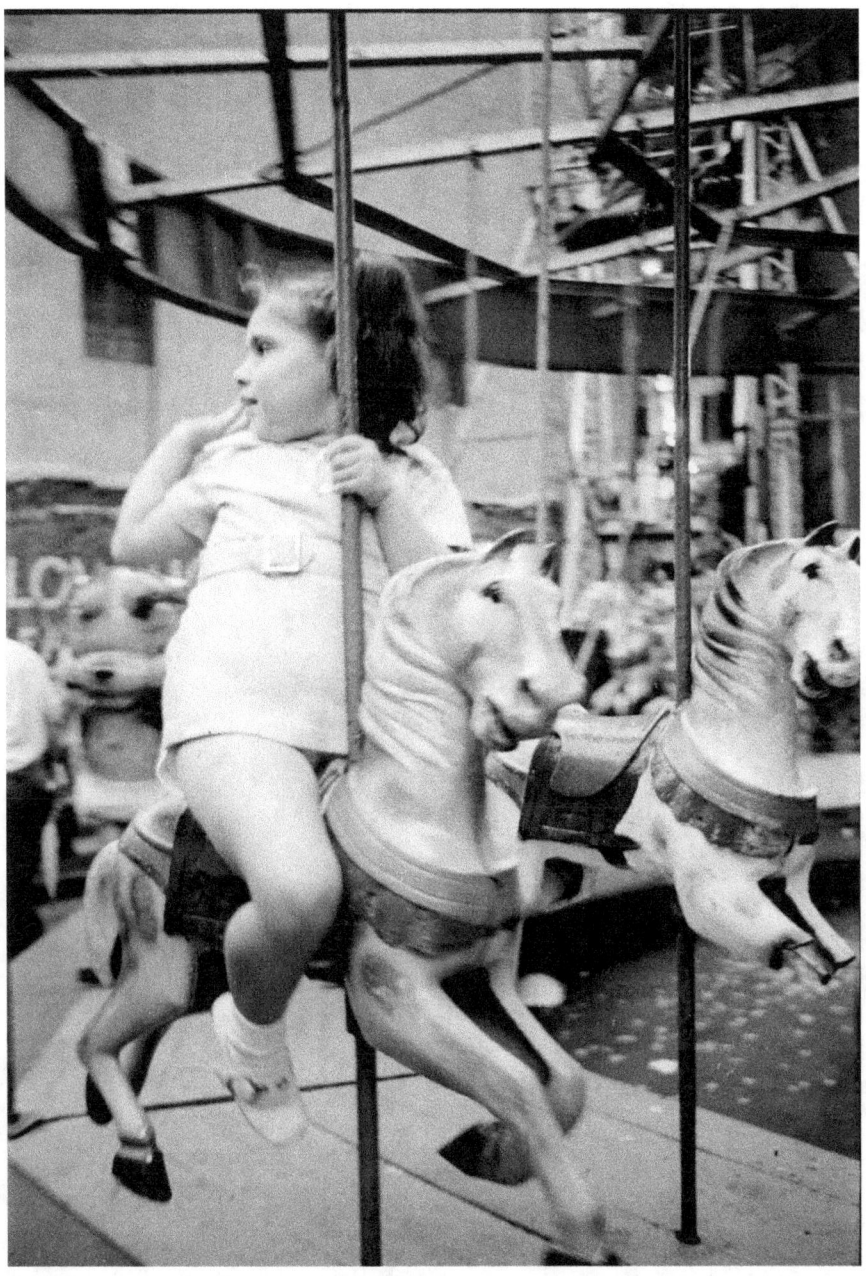

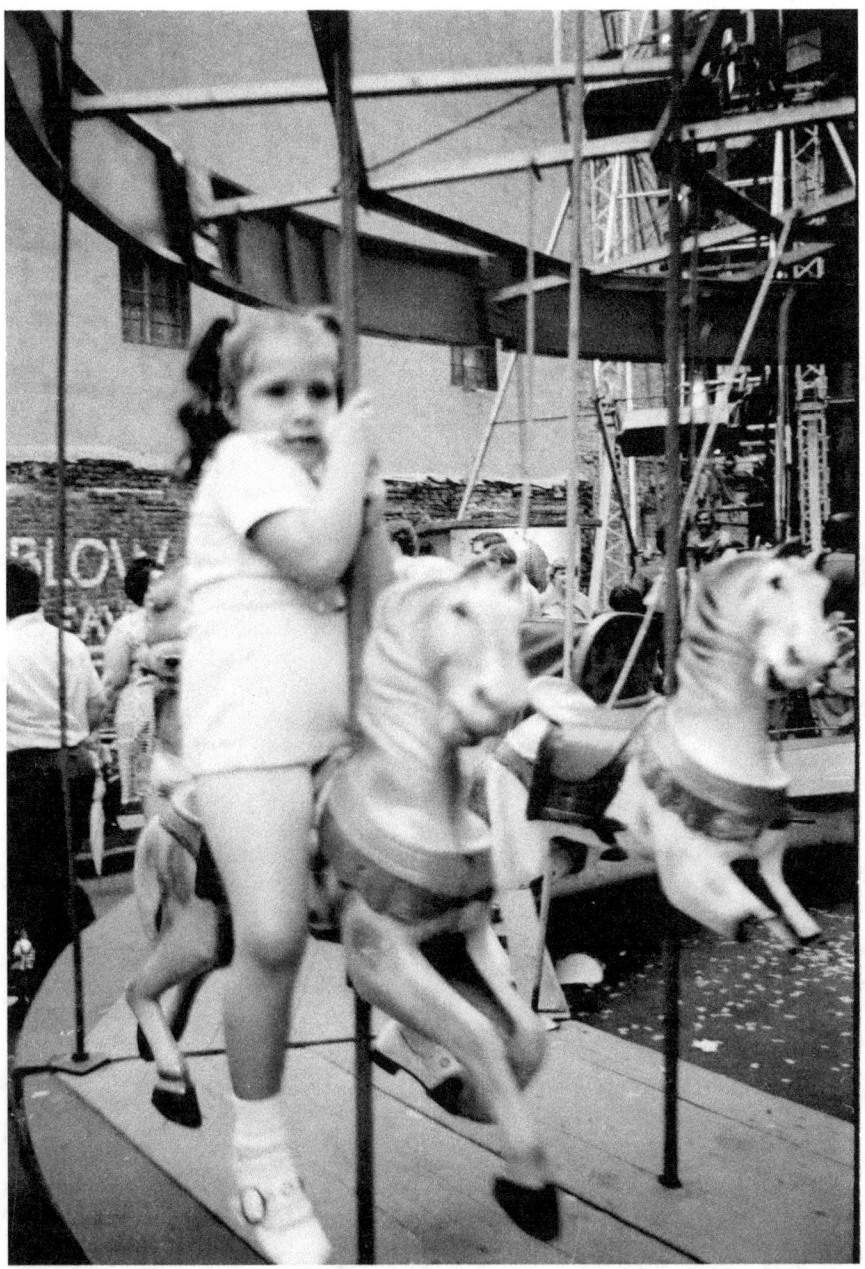

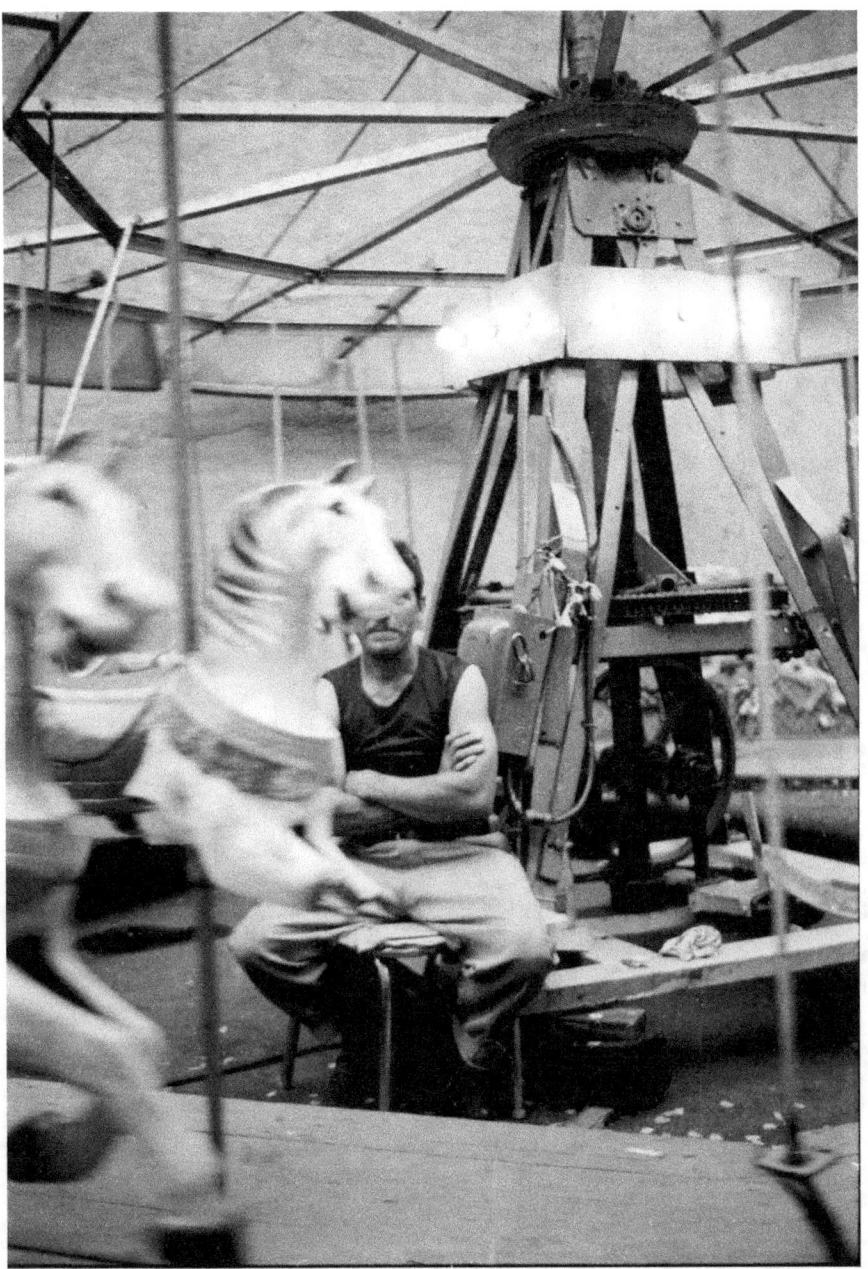

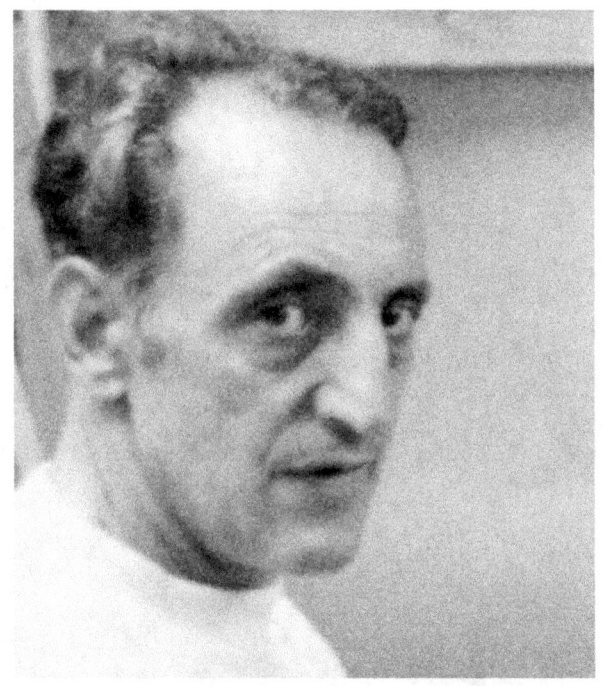

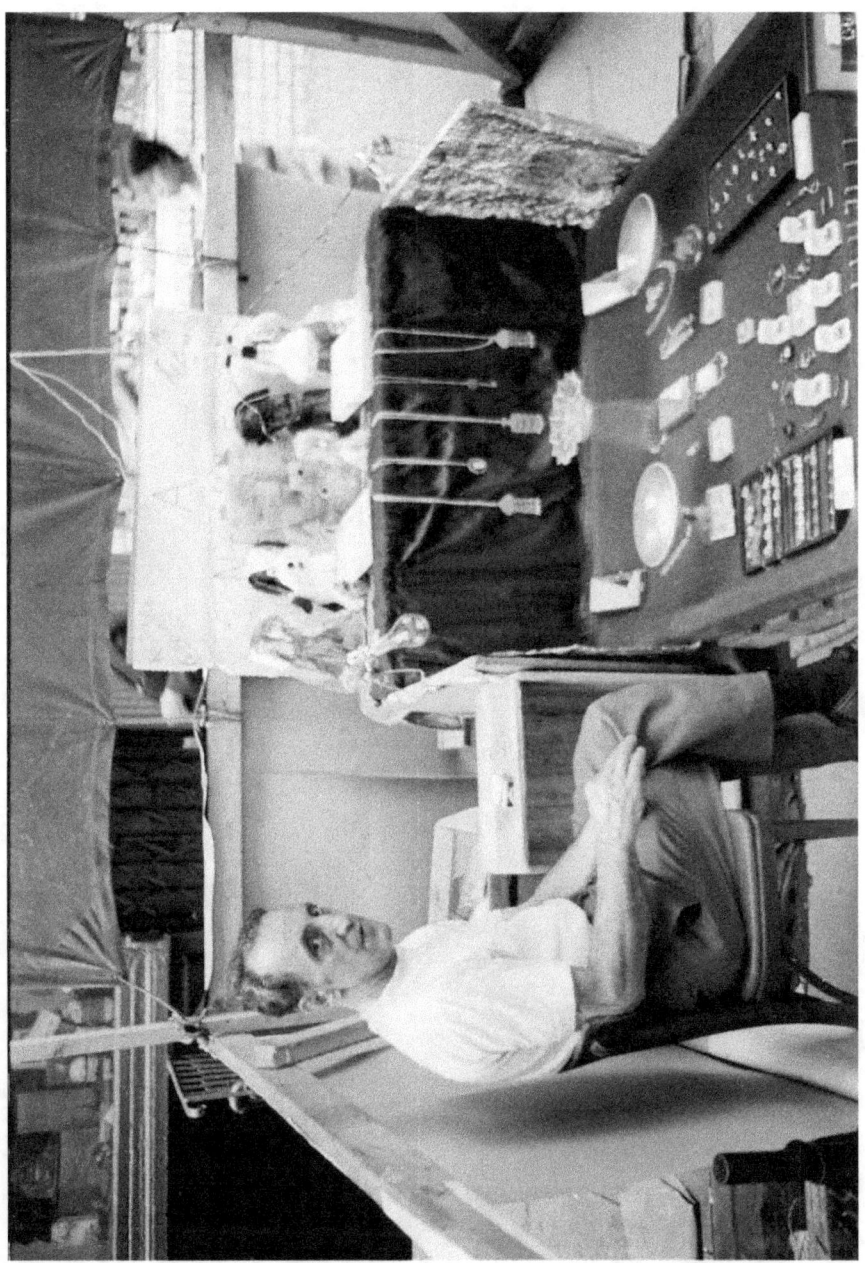

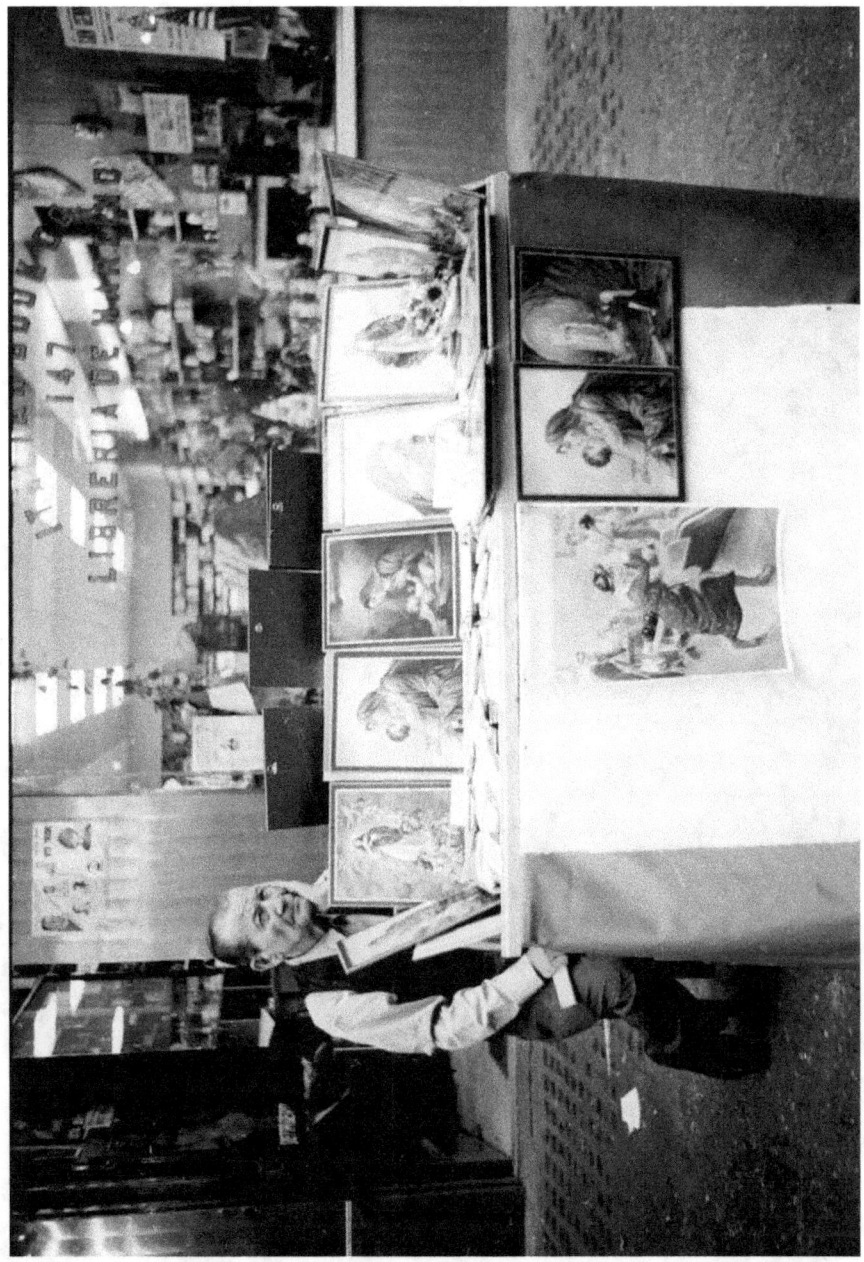

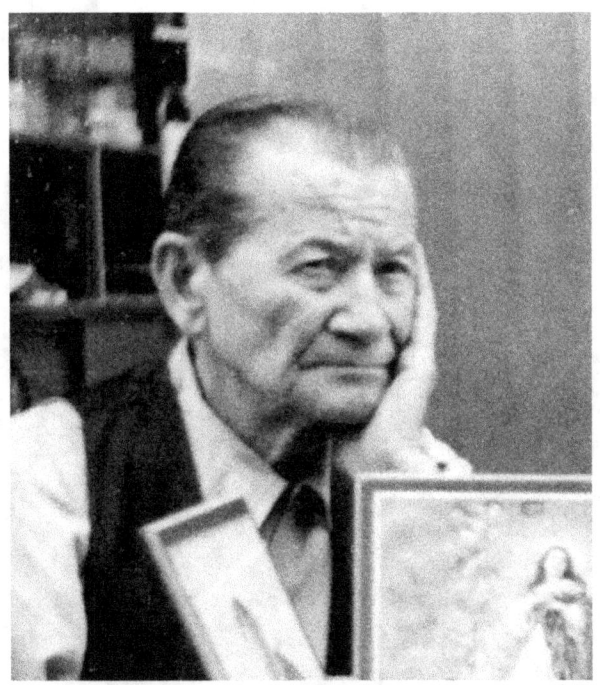

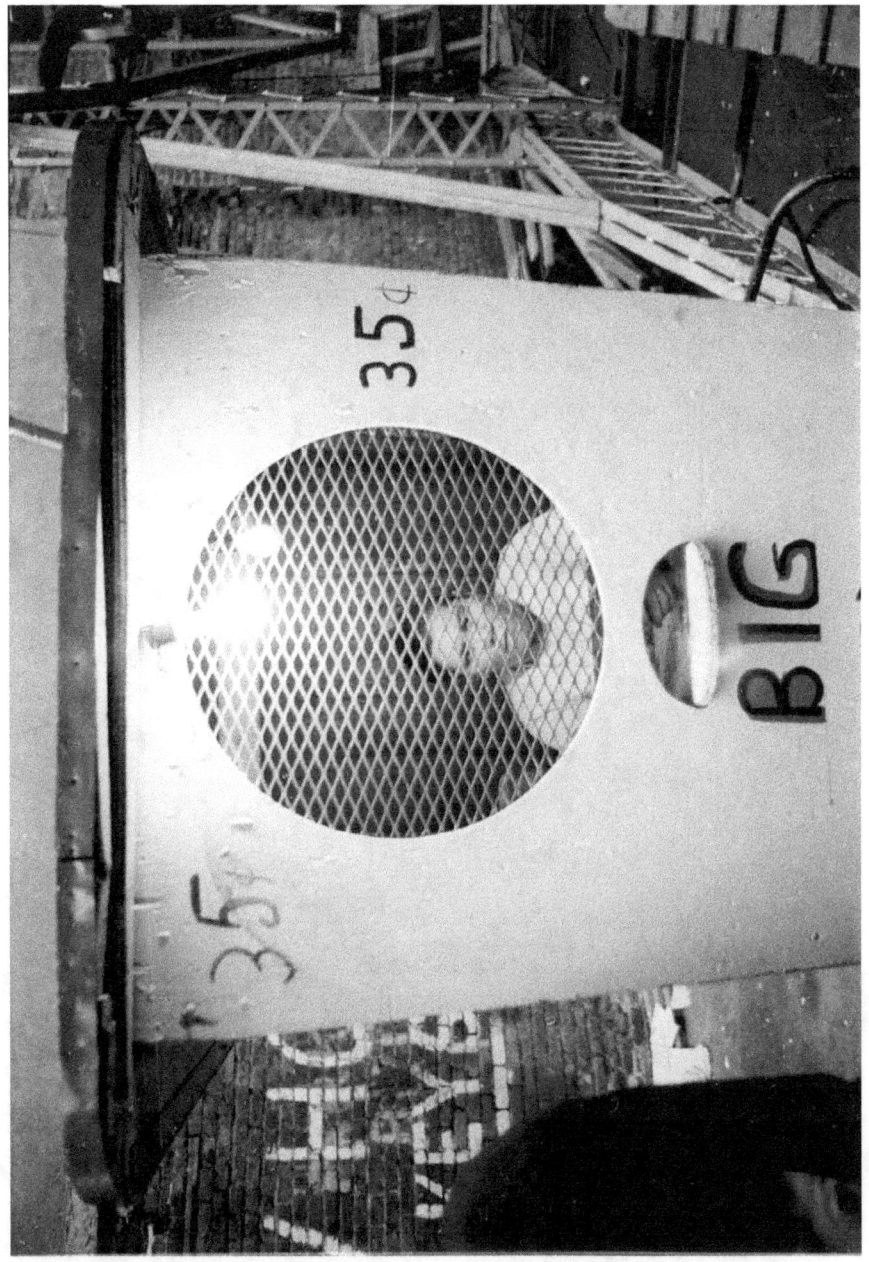

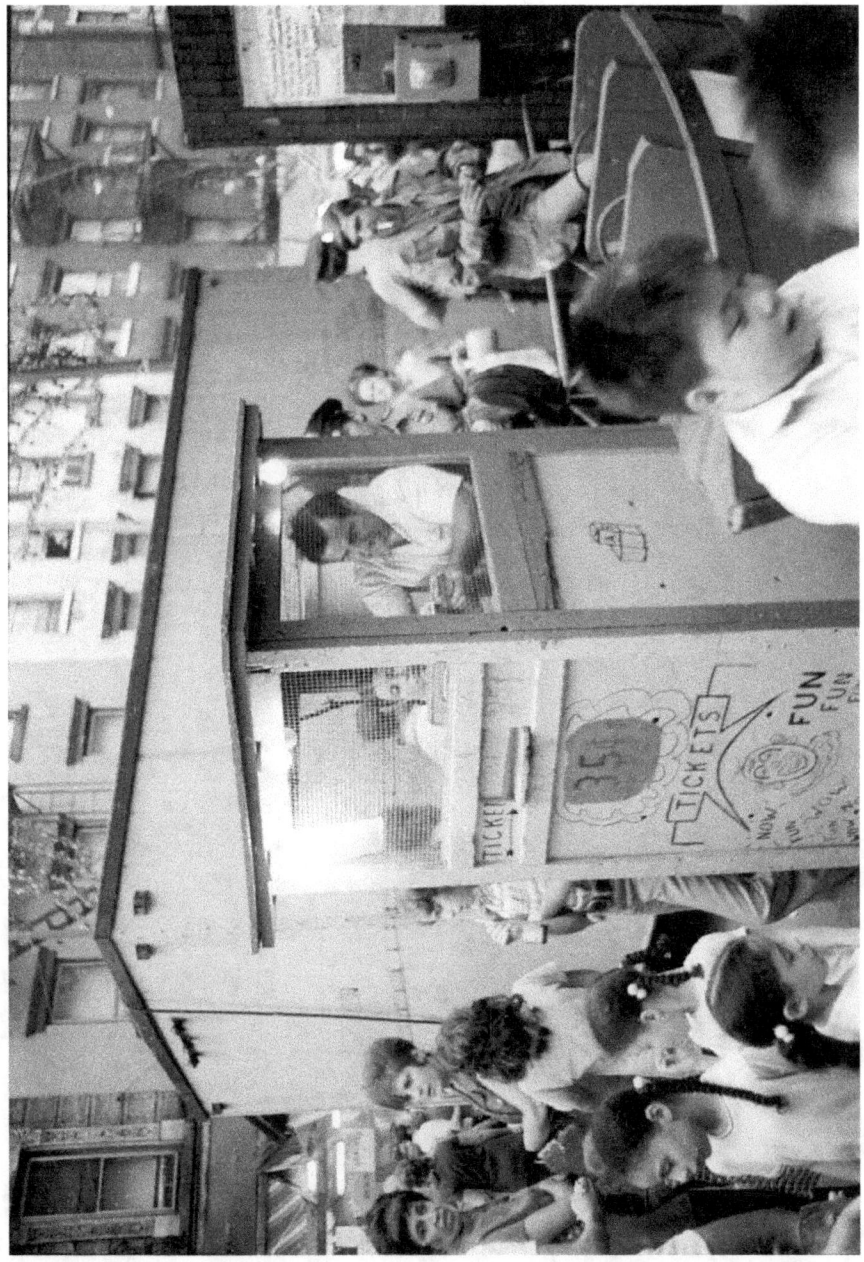

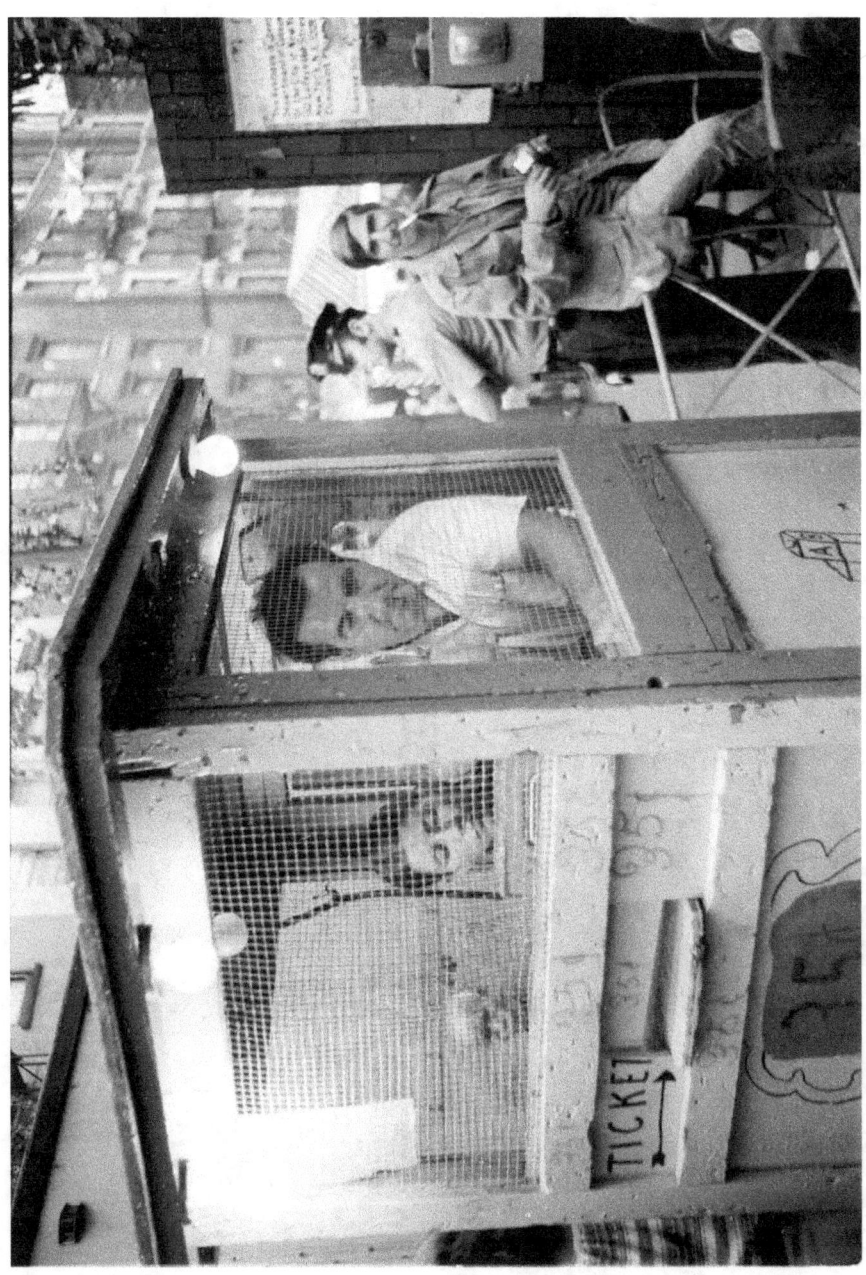

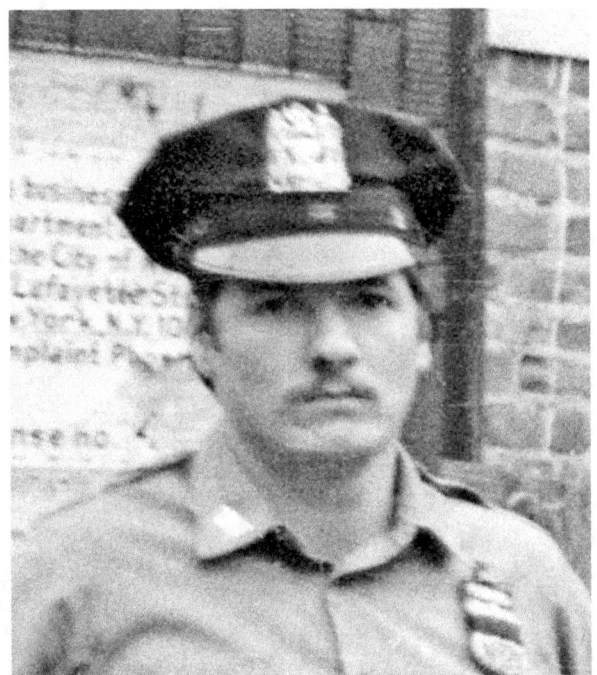

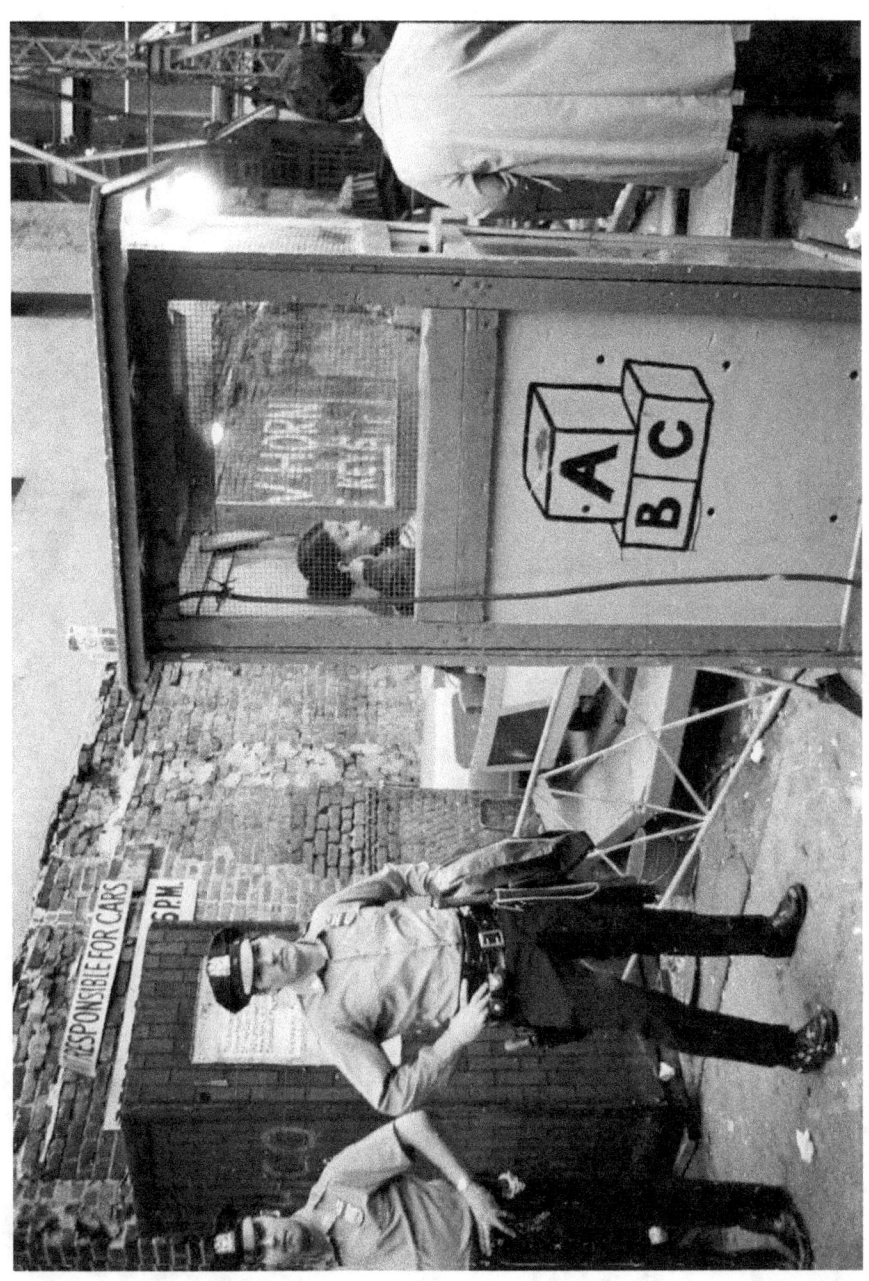

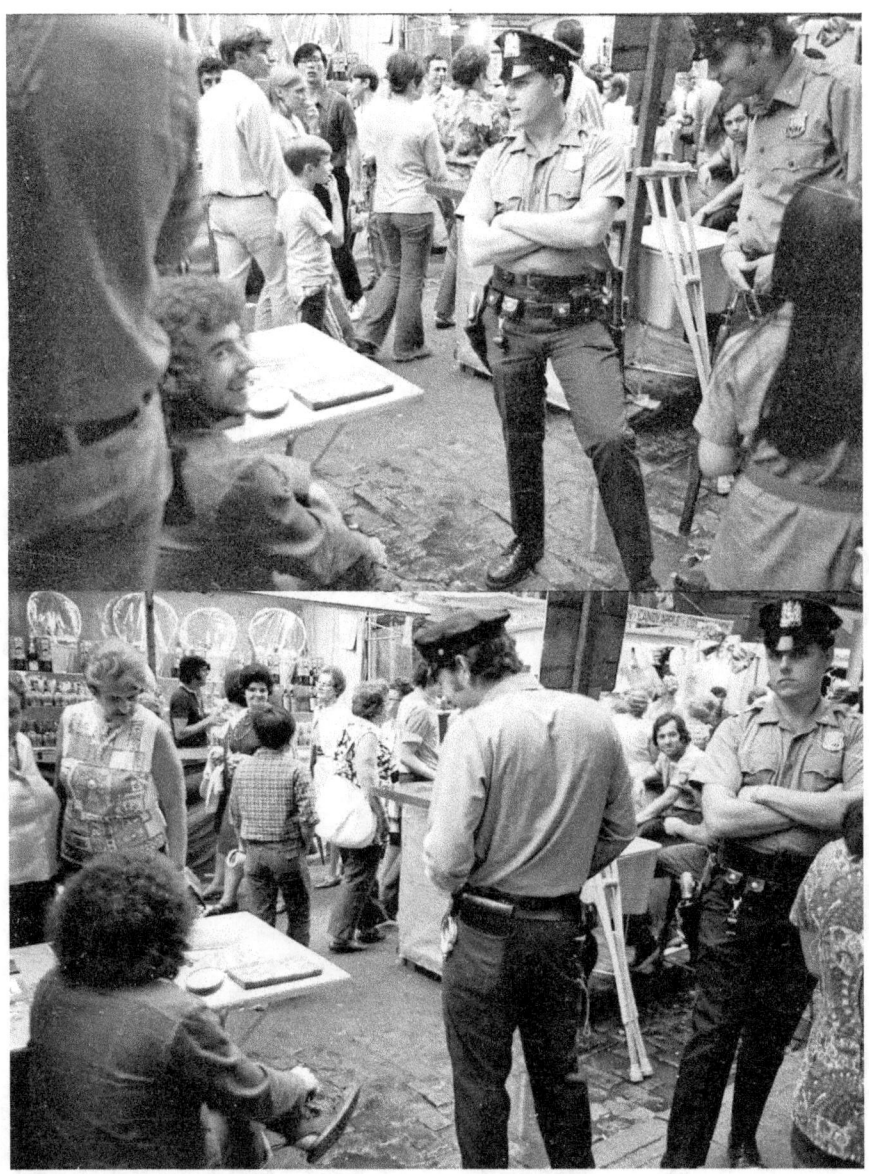

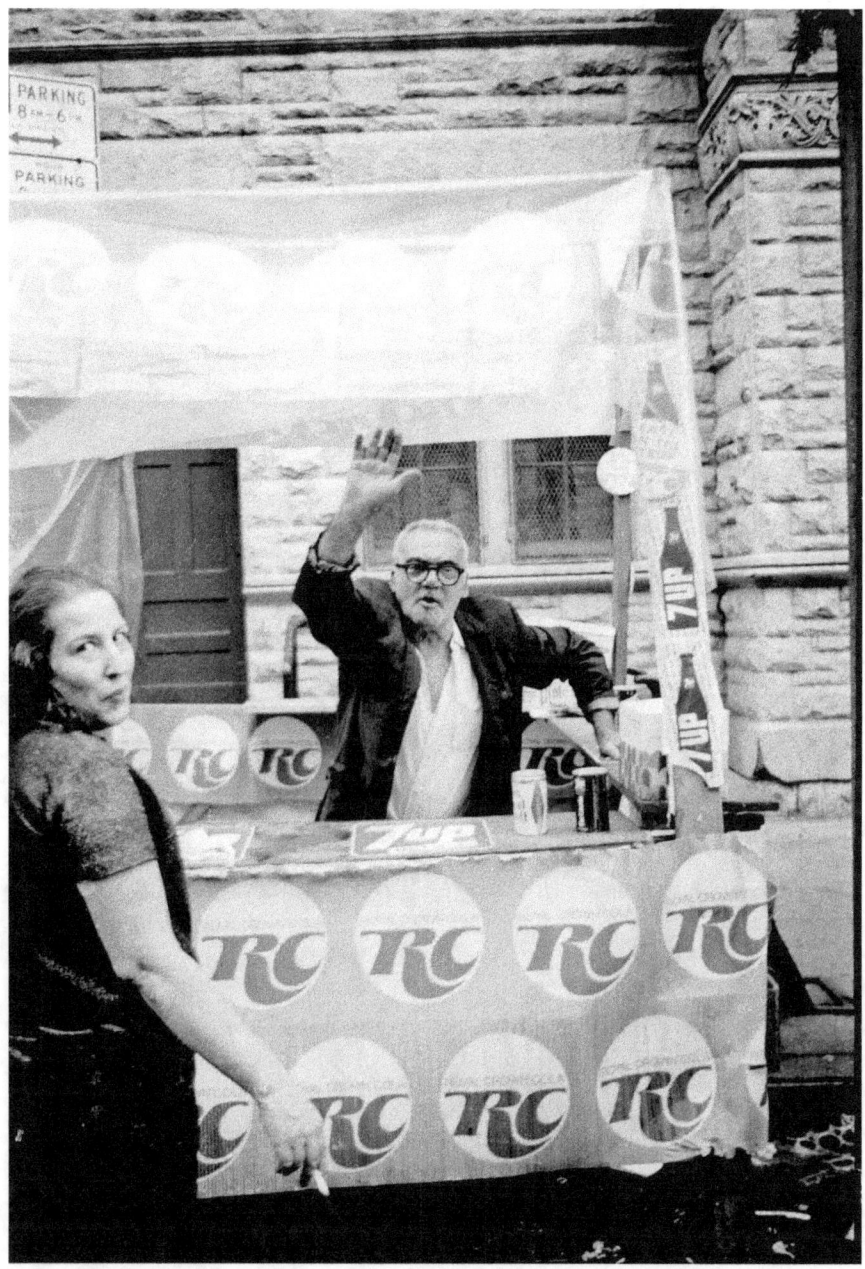

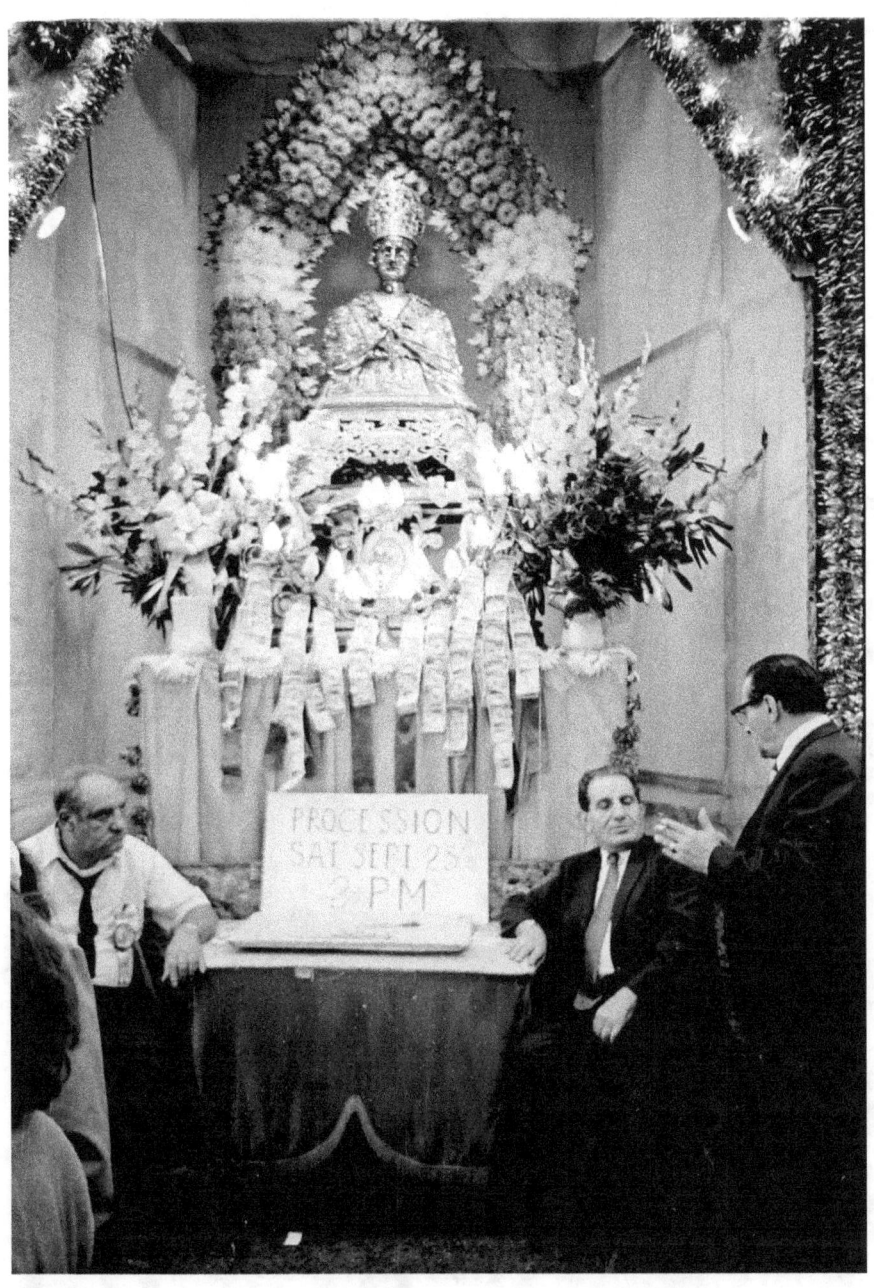

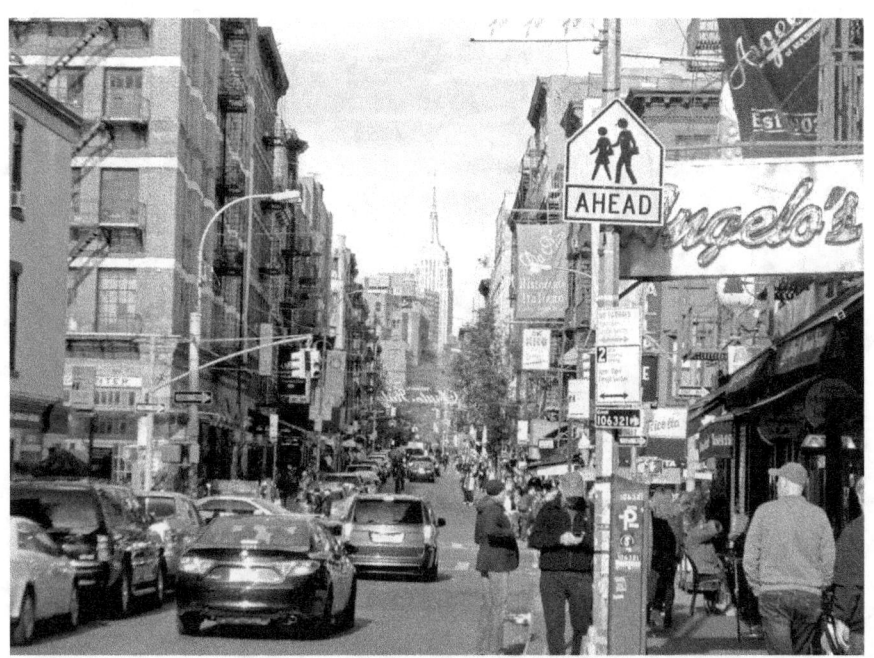

November 4, 2017
Mulberry Street, New York City

Other Books by Alan Pakaln

La Festa di San Gennaro

Italian translation of
*The Feast of San Gennaro,
Little Italy, New York, 1971*

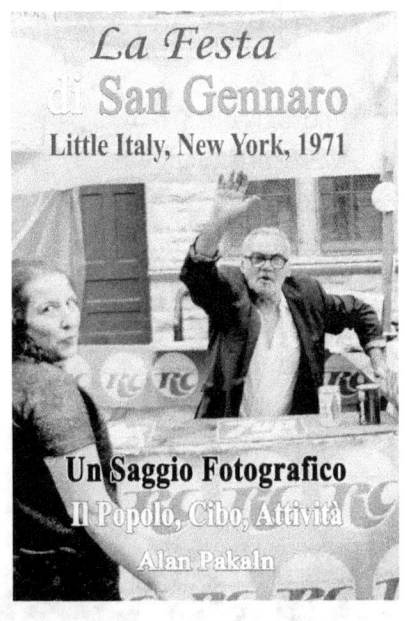

*New York Shadow:
Behind The Scenes*

Eight series
1965 through 2018
New York City
Color and B&W

Coated paper
Quality printing

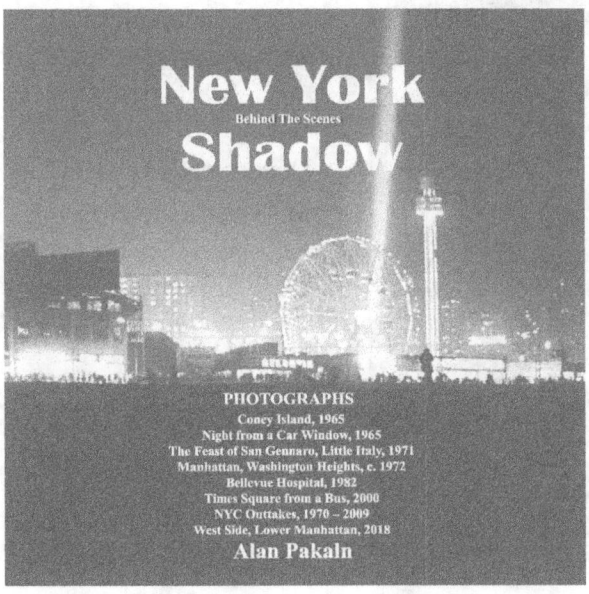

NYC: B&W
Photographs, 1965-2018

Photographs from
New York Shadow
All B&W
Uncoated paper
Standard printing
Priced accordingly

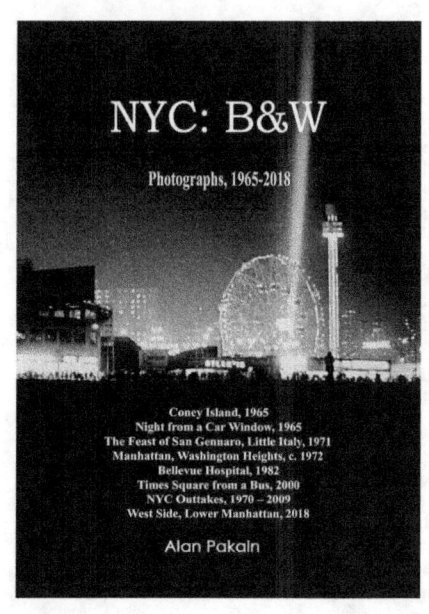

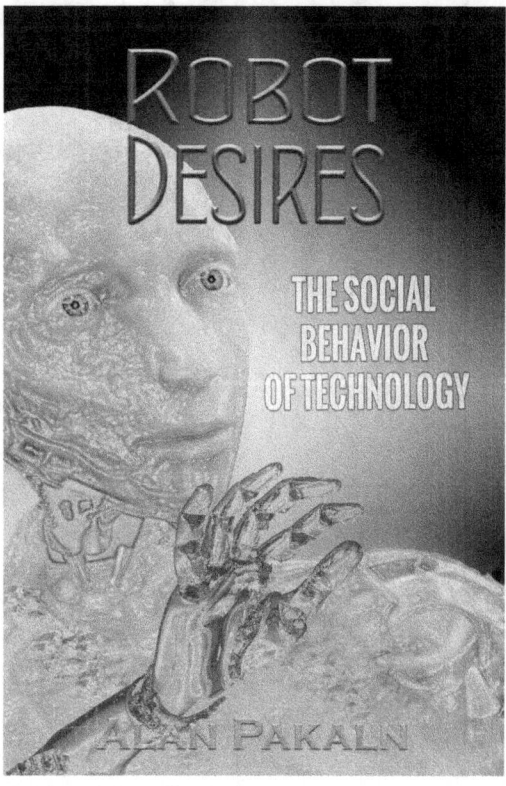

Robot Desires:
The Social Behavior
of Technology

AKA:
"Invention Is The Mother
of Necessity"

Technology itself is driving
the direction of our inventions.
Literally.

And will drive some of us
toward new communities,
e.g. cohousing.

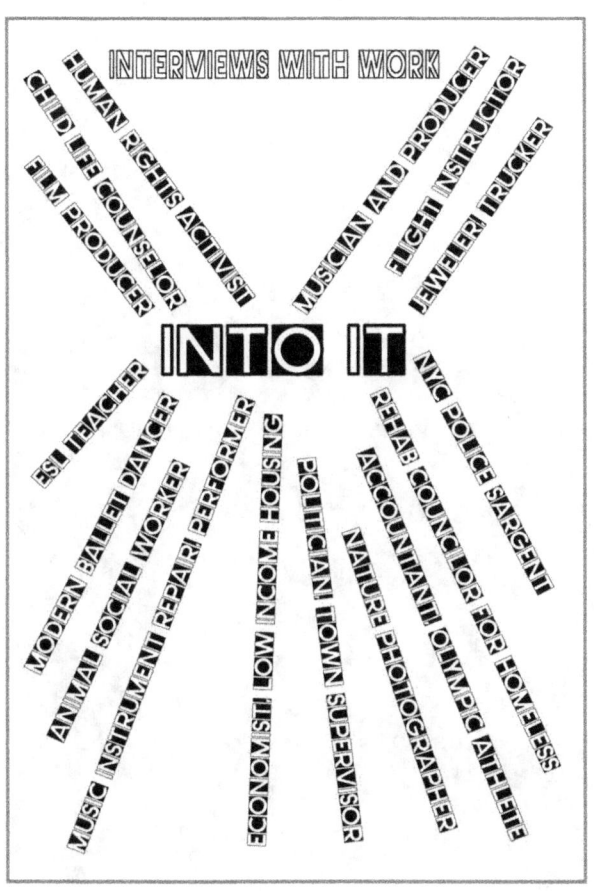

Into It:
Interviews With Work

Transcripts from recorded interviews:

16 personal views, from a South Bronx police sergeant, to a female flight instructor, and an Olympian athlete slash accountant.